Proverbi siciliani/Sicilian Proverbs

Library of Congress Cataloging-in-Publication Data

Proverbi Siciliani/Sicilian Proverbs / [compiled by] Arthur V. Dieli ; illustrations by Carlo Puleo.
    pages cm. -- (Sicilian Studies ; Volume XXVIII)
    ISBN 1-881901-98-X (pbk.)
    1. Proverbs, Italian--Italy--Sicily--Translations into English. 2. Sicily (Italy)--Social life and customs. I. Dieli, Arthur V., 1927- II. Puleo, Carlo.
    PN6475.S5P76 2014
    398.951'09458--dc23
                 2014003447

Acknowledgements
The publisher is grateful to Arba Sicula for a generous grant that in part made the publication of this book possible.
The illustration on the cover entitled "Il nostro sentiero" is from Carlo Puleo's *La Pittura dal 1958 al 1998*, Palermo, Thule, 1998.

For information and for orders, write to:

Legas

P.O. Box 149
Mineola, New York
11501, USA

3 Wood Aster Bay
Ottawa, Ontario
K2R 1D3 Canada

legaspublishing.com

Arthur V. Dieli

Proverbi siciliani/ Sicilian Proverbs

Illustrations by
Carlo Puleo

LEGAS

Legas

Sicilian Studies

Volume XXVIII

Series Editor: Gaetano Cipolla

Other Volumes Published in this Series:

Acknowledgements

I owe thanks to many people without whom I could never have accomplished this work. First of all my parents who spoke to us in Sicilian during our childhood. Gratuitously enriching our lives. That early language, long forgotten was reawakened in me when my daughter Paula gave me a book of Sicilian proverbs on her return from a trip to Sicily. I found them delightful and entertaining and decided to eventually try my hand at translating them into English. Thanks to Arba Sicula I learned about Joseph Bellestri's *Sicilian-English* and *English-Sicilian* dictionaries which I ordered once I decided to take on the project. Bellestri edited my first batch of proverbs, and that encouraged me to continue. Danny Sutera, who was born in Alcamo, gave me some proverbs he had learned from his mother. On one trip to Sicily I picked up a reprint of Antonino Traina's *Vocabolario Siciliano-Italiano,* from which I've drawn many proverbs. The bibliography lists other books that I've drawn from, but the majority of the proverbs come from the works of folklorist Giuseppe Pitrè (1841-1916). Thanks also to Charlie Giordano, an Arba Sicula member who edited the English translations, and helped me clarify some of the meanings. I must also thank the members of Arba Sicula who encouraged me to publish the proverbs and I especially thank Gaetano Cipolla the President and Editor of Arba Sicula without whom this book could not have happened.

The illustrations in the book and on the cover are the work of the renowned Sicilian artist, sculptor, poet and writer Carlo Puleo. I am thrilled that he agreed to illustrate the book. It seems fitting that the proverbs, which are such an integral part of Sicily's culture should be accompanied by the work of one of its most eminent artists.

Abbreviations

adj.	adjective
adv.	adverb
aug.	augmentative
bot.	botanical
conj.	conjunction
dim.	diminutive
excl.	exclamation
fut.	future
ichth.	ichthyology
imp.	imperative
inv.	invariable
lit.	literally
loc.	locative
n.f.	feminine noun
n.f.pl.	feminine plural noun
n.m.	masculine
noun p.pl.	person plural
p.sing.	person singular
past p.	past participle
pejor.	pejorative
pl.	plural
prep.	preposition
pres.p.	present participle
pron.	pronoun
refl.	reflexive
subj.	subjunctive
Tr.	translator
v.i.	intransitive verb
v.t.	transitive verb
zool.	zoological

Introduction

This collection of Sicilian proverbs is a small sampling from many sources. The major source is Giuseppe Pitrè's four volume work, *Proverbi Siciliani: Raccolti E Confrontati Con Quelli Degli Altri Dialetti D' Italia*, 1870. A secondary source of many proverbs is Antonino Traina's *Vocabolario Siciliano - Italiano*, 1868. Proverbs were also drawn from many other sources, all of which are listed in the bibliography.

The proverbs are in alphabetic order by headword, or keyword, terms I use interchangeably. Variations in spelling are not unusual in Sicilian. Where differences were encountered, the spelling used in the proverb is retained even when the spelling chosen for the headword was the one preferred by Traina or Piccitto in their dictionaries. When the same proverb is handled differently by different sources, both versions are included. Alaimo and Traina sometimes transcribe a proverb as one sentence, when Pitrè shows it as two. In those cases the Pitrè version was used whenever it was available to me. I tried to carefully retain the variations in spellings contained within the proverbs that Pitrè collected from the many different parts of Sicily. Sometimes Pitrè included the place name within the proverb as in the following example.

A tempu di còcciu, si dormi ccu 'n' occhiu (***Chiaramonte***).
At harvest time you sleep with one eye open.

Whenever Pitrè follows a proverb with an explanation in Italian, its english translation usually follows the proverb. You'll see an example of this in the **lavuri** headword. Quotation marks were used to indicate a close translation of his explanation, rather than the usual free translation. Sometimes Pitrè's Italian text is included, followed by my translation. You'll find an example under the **caiccu** headword. Other authors, notably Isidoro Copani and Sandro Attanasio provided extensive commentary for many of the proverbs and sayings in their collections, but I have not attempted to include them.

Some proverbs are open to more than one meaning. This is especially the case when the vocabulary itself has more than one meaning. In those cases I've relied on the meanings offered by native Sicilians such as Pitrè, Traina, Attanasio, and Copani, as well as others. When a native Sicilian explanation was lacking, and I felt that the meaning was unclear, I followed my own translation with a literal, word for word translation. I owe my understanding of Sicilian to my early childhood, growing up in a

Sicilian-American household. My parents, who were from Caltagirone in the province of Catania, usually spoke with us in Sicilian and they used Italian or English when we had visitors who were not Sicilian.

The lyrical beauty of a Sicilian proverb is best appreciated in its original. This is especially the case when the Sicilian version includes a rhyme.

> Quannu l'acidduzzi 'un fannu dannu,
> È signu ca cuntrariu avisti l'annu.
> *If the birds haven't messed*
> *The year hasn't been the best.*

On rare occasions, as in the above example, the English translation also includes a rhyme.

Sometimes the Sicilian rhyme is nicely matched by the English version in both meaning and rhyme:

> Prestu, tintu.
> *Haste makes waste.*

It may be that sometimes the rhyme is the only reason for the existence of the proverb, as in this example. On the other hand this may be an example of a proverb whose meaning has eluded me.

> Pani asciuttu fa bon fruttu.
> *Dry bread makes good fruit.*

Dry bread could stand for a hard life and good fruit could mean that you became stronger for it.

Now and then the tables are turned and the rhyme is only in the English version For example:

> Quannu la gatta nun cc'è, li surci abballanu.
> *When the cat's away the mice will play.*

While not literally word for word, many of the Sicilian proverbs in Pitrè's collection have very close equivalents in our own culture.

> Purtari lignu a lu voscu.
> *Carrying coals to Newcastle.*
> *Lit. Carrying wood to the forest.*

Pitrè organized his collection of some 13,000 proverbs into ninety chapters, grouped by subject. The first eighty-seven chapters are alphabetized by the first word of the chapter title; from Chapter I, *Abitudine, Usanze* to Chapter LXXXVII *Vizi, Mali Abiti.* Within the chapters the proverbs are alphabetized by the first and succeeding words of the proverb itself. Attanasio also organized his collection into chapters by subject. His sixty-three chapters range from *Abbondanza* to *Vendetta.* Annaro also organized his proverb collection by subject and wrote using the parlata of Caltagirone.

This English translation is organized by keyword because my primary interest is to make Sicilian vocabulary accessible to English speakers, letting the content of the proverb serve as an example of the use of the keyword. Similarly, in his *Vocabolario Siciliano - Italiano,* Traina quotes proverbs as examples of the usage of the headword he is defining. In defining the word *mircanti* on page 596, Traina includes seven proverbs as examples of its use. In defining *pani* on pages 691,2 Traina includes twenty-five proverbs as examples of its use. Thus, he is using the proverbs to give Italian speakers some examples of the use of the Sicilian word. Copani also organized his collection by keyword.

It is often said that the proverbs give us a window into Sicilian culture. As true as that statement may be, it is also true that each proverb has a date of origin and the culture it reflects may no longer exist. This is readily apparent with proverbs about the now practically extinct Sicilian donkey. It is not so readily apparent with some other proverbs. Here's an example of one whose usage may become obsolete.

> Figghi tardii, orfani primintii.
> *Late children, early orphans.*

As our life span increases parents are still here to see their late born children reach adulthood. Some are even seeing their great-grandchildren. But the proverb surely reflected the culture of the time.

In America we're familiar with many of the proverbs Benjamin Franklin published in Poor Richard's Almanac. Here are a few of them.

> A penny saved is a penny earned.
> Hunger is the best pickle.
> When you taste honey, remember gall.
> A good example is the best sermon.
> A man in a passion rides a mad horse.

In Sicilian culture proverbs are similarly used. This one encourages healthy living habits.

Cu' havi un pedi a lu burdellu, nn'havi n'àutru a San Bartulumeu.
He who frequents the brothel will soon end up at St. Bartholomew's.

San Bartulemeu was a hospital for incurables dedicated to the care of those suffering with syphilis.

This proverb warns against trusting carelessly.

Nu nni putemu fidari mancu di ddu patri chi nni fici.
We can't even trust in the father that made us.

Similar to Poor Richard's *Hunger is the best pickle,* is this Sicilian one.

Nun cc' è megghiu sarsa di la fami.
There's no better sauce than hunger.

The Sicilian version of Poor Richard's *A man in a passion rides a mad horse* is:

Dici Platuni: La passioni vinci la raggiuni.
Plato says: passion overcomes reason.

The universal concern with procrastination, the failure to understand that we should celebrate our mistakes, that perfection is not possible, is nicely expressed in this Sicilian proverb:

Lu fattu è nnimicu di lu pirfettu.
Deeds are the enemies of perfect.

The Sicilian sense of realism is encapsulated in this next proverb.

La fama vola.
A good name is a sometime thing.

One of the comments that Pitrè sometimes adds to a proverb is that he heard this proverb on such and such an occasion. This highlights the fact that many of the proverbs are in use in everyday Sicilian conversation. He also comments when including a proverb that he has never heard used. In such cases, he cites the collection from which the proverb was taken. You'll find examples of both cases cited in this small collection.

Pitrè also drew on many other sources for his collection of Sicilian proverbs. He lists thirty-six of those sources in a bibliography in Volume I. In a second bibliography he lists twenty-six sources for proverbs from other Italian regions and provinces as well as one French listing and another in German, from which he draws examples to compare and contrast with the Sicilian version.

From time to time one proverb or another seems to be my favorite. Here's one from that group of favorites:

L'omu sempri apprenni e mori gnuranti.
Man is always learning and dies ignorant.

I've approached the task of translation with a sense of excitement and respect. I've tried to produce an honest piece of work but I'm sure I've made more than my share of errors, from simple typographical to profound. I will not be surprised to learn that I have misinterpreted the meaning of some words and proverbs.

Lu fattu è nnimicu di lu pirfettu.
Deeds are the enemies of perfect.

Proverbi siciliani / Sicilian Proverbs

abbajari *v.i.* bark, shout inconsiderately, ask for in vain.
A un povir' omu, ogni cani cci abbaja. Source: Pitrè, I, 251.
Eng. Every dog barks at a wretched man.

Cani abbaia e voi pasci. Source: Pitrè, I, 123.
Eng. Dogs bark and oxen graze.

Luna e cavaddu nun curanu l'abbajari di li cani. Source: Pitrè, II, 402.
Eng. Neither the moon nor the horse pay attention to the barking of dogs.

abballanu *v.i.* dance.
Quannu la gatta 'un cc' è, li surci abballanu. Source: Pitrè, II, 59.
Eng. When the cat's away the mice will play.

abballari *v.i.* dance. *Also: **ballari.***
Abballa mentri furtuna sona. Source: Pitrè, III, 371.
Eng. Make hay while the sun shines.
Lit. Dance while luck is playing.

abbanniari *v.t.* advertise, publicize, auction, announce banns.
Lu putiaru zocc'havi abbannia. Source: Pitrè, I, 321.
Eng. The shopkeeper hawks what he has.

abbasta *adv.* enough, sufficiently.
Abbasta un sulu pazzu pri casa. Source: Pitrè, IV, 49.
Eng. One madman is enough per household.

Lu pocu abbasta, l'assai suverchia. Source: Pitrè, IV, 122.
Eng. A little is enough, a lot is overmuch.

abbati *n.m.* abbot.
Comu canta l'abbati, arrispunni lu sagristanu. Source: Pitrè, II, 336.
Eng. The sacristan follows the abbot's lead.
Tr. note: This proverb is in Pitrè, Volume II, Chapter 46, Government, Laws, National Interest.

La missa cantata si paga; l'assistenti si paganu; pri lu sagristanu nun cci bastanu li dinari (**Monreale**). Source: Pitrè, II, 354.
Eng. *The sung mass is to be paid for, the assistants are to be paid; for the sacristan the money is never enough.*
Tr. note: This proverb is in Pitrè, Volume II, Chapter 48, Earnings, Wages.

abbèniri *v.i.* happen, occur. *Also:* **avvèniri.**
Prestu e beni, di raru avveni. Source: Pitrè, III, 367.
Eng. *Haste and doing good rarely go together.*

abbilità *n.f.* ability. *Also:* **abbilitati.**
Tri cosi cci vonu ad arricchiri: un picca, un assai, un nenti: picca dinari, assai abbilità, nenti cuscenza. Source: Pitrè, II, 285.
Eng. *Three things are needed to get rich: a little, a lot, a nothing: little money, much ability, no conscience.*

abbintari *v.t.* rest, calm, cease, stop.
Simina terra abbintata, ma no terra vantata. Source: Pitrè, I, 66.
Eng. *Seed fallow land rather than the acclaimed and much used land.*

abbitu, *n.m.* dress, religious habit; habit; bot. pine tree (Pinus Picea Linné)
Also: **abitu.**
Spissu sutta abbitu vili si trova cori gentili. Source: Traina, 5.
Eng. *A gentle heart is often found under tattered clothes.*

abbozzari *v.t.* put up with, let slide. *Also:* ***abbuzzari***.
Cu' è 'mpiatu, o abbozza o mori dispiratu. Source: Pitrè, I, 82.
Eng. *Learn to put up with the small stuff.*
Lit. *An employee. either puts up with things or dies of desperation.*

abbrazzari *v.t.* embrace, hug.
Cui troppu abbrazza, nenti strinci. Source: Pitrè, IV, 119.
Eng. *Jack of all trades and master of none.*
Lit. *He who embraces too much. ends up with nothing.*

abbruciari *v.t.* burn.
Quannu la casa s'abbrucia, jèttacci ligna. Source: Bellantonio, II, 108.
Eng. *Don't waste your time on a lost cause.*
Lit. *When the house is aflame, throw on more wood.*

Si nun ti voi abbruciari nun ti mettiri accantu a lu focu. Source: Traina, 394.
Eng. *If you can't stand the heat. get out of the kitchen.*
Lit. *If you don't want to get burned, don't get near the fire.*

La bona facci parturisci amici,
La viritati abbrusca comu pici. Source: Pitrè, IV, 57.
Eng. *A smile makes friends,*
The truth burns like pitch.

abbuscari *v.t.* procure, find, obtain, earn, get.
Cu' accarizza li muli abbusca cauci. Source: Pitrè, II, 345.
Eng. *When you help an ingrate, don't expect thanks.*
Lit. *He who caresses mules gets kicked.*
Tr. note: This proverb is in Pitrè, Volume II, Chapter 47, Gratitude, Ingratitude.

accattari *v.t.* buy.

Accatta scecchi e vinni scecchi. Source: Pitrè, I, 308.
Eng. *Stick with what you know.*
Lit. *Buy donkeys and sell donkeys.*

'Un accattari la gatta 'ntra lu saccu. Source: Pitrè, III, 297.
Eng. *Don't buy a pig in a poke.*
Lit. *Don't buy a cat in a sack.*

accetta *n.f.* hatchet.
L'accetta fa l' arvulu. Source: Pitrè, I, 61.
Eng. *A pruned tree grows better.*

acchianari *v.t.* climb, increase.
La virtù è 'na bedda picciotta e tutti l'amanu, ma pochi 'n casa cci acchiananu. Source: Pitrè, IV, 146.
Eng. *Virtue is a beautiful young woman that everyone loves, but few can climb to her house.*

accuminzari *v.t.* to begin, to start, to commence.
Cosa beni accuminzata è menza finuta. Source: Pitrè, III, 374.
Eng. *A task well started is already half finished.*

Cui vecchiu voli campari, a bon' ura voli accuminzari. Source: Bellantonio, II, 211.
Eng. *If you want to live to an old age, you need to start early.*
Tr. note: Another example of the Sicilian sense of humor.

accupari *v.t.* hide, cover, gasp.
Quannu funci nascinu, tanta terra accùpanu. Source: Pitrè, IV, 213.
Eng. *When mushrooms sprout, they cover much ground.*

accussì *adv.* thus, this way, so, as.
Cu' pò nun vò, cu' vò nun pò, cu' fa nun sa e cu' sa nun fa, e 'cussi tuttu lu munnu va. Source: Traina, 787.
Eng. *He who can, won't; who wants to, can't; who does it, doesn't know how; and who knows how, doesn't do it; and that's the way of the world.*

acidduzzi *n.m.pl. dim.* little birds.
Quannu l'acidduzzi 'un fannu dannu,
È signu ca cuntrariu avisti l'annu. Source: Pitrè, I, 59.

Eng. *The year hasn't been the best,*
If the birds haven't messed.

acqua *n.f.* water, rain.
Acqua di primintiu,
Allarga l'armu miu;
Acqua e suli 'ntra li simenzi,
Mi criscinu li spiranzi;
Acqua di maju e aprili,
Curru cu tutti li vili;
Poi boni matinati,
Ricchizza di li casi. (**Borgetto**). Source: Pitrè, I, 26.
Eng. *Early rain,*
Cheers my soul;
Water and sun during seeding,
Inspires hope;
April and May night rains,
I run with sails unfurled;
Then good mornings,
Will enrich the houses.
Pitrè explains that excessive humidity at night or in the morning, as the grain is maturing, could stunt its growth. He adds that the proverb is recited by those farmers whose lives depend on the crop.

Acqui chi taci vilinusa tagghia. Source: Pitrè, IV, 67.
Eng. *The person who keeps to himself warrants concern.*
Lit. *Quiet waters cut poisonously.*

Sempri fu vilinusa l'acqua morta. Source: Pitrè, IV, 67.
Eng. *Be wary of the person who fails to engage in open conversation.*
Lit. *Stagnant waters have always been deadly.*

adaciu *adv.* slowly, softly, gently.
Adaciu adaciu si fa gran viaggiu.
Eng. *A long journey begins with a single step.*
Lit. *With slow and steady steps you can travel far.*

addannàrisi *v.t.* be damned, lead to hell.
Li dinari fannu addannari. Source: Pitrè, III, 264.
Eng. *Money is the root of all evil.*
Lit. *Money leads to hell.*

addimura *v.i.* delay, hesitate, protest.
Cani ch'addimura, porta caccia. Source: Pitrè, I, 123.
Eng. *The dog that's late is bringing the catch.*

addivintari *v.i.* become.
Si vôi riccu addivintari, 'nsignati a travagghiari. Source: Pitrè, III, 212.
Eng. *If you want to become rich, learn to work.*

Si vôi riccu addivintari, 'nsignati a sparagnari Source: Pitrè, III, 212.
Eng. *If you want to become rich, learn to save.*

addugari *v.t.* to rent, hire, accomodate.
Lu sennu non si vendi nè s'adduga.
Eng. *Wisdom is not sold, nor can it be rented.*

affàcciu *adv.* at sight, agri. without plowing.
Cui simina affàcciu, meti a lu strafàcciu. Source: Pitrè, I, 40.
Eng. *Who sows on unplowed ground has nothing to harvest.*

affannatu *n.m.* anguish, distress, trouble, affliction, pain.
Vôi fari parrari lu mutu? lèvacci lu sô affannatu. Source: Pitrè, II, 285.
Eng. *If you want to make the mute speak get rid of his affliction.*

affari *n.m.* business, matter, chore.
Dissi la vacca a lu voi:
Ognunu sapi l'affari soi. Source: Pitrè, IV, 164.
Eng. *Said the cow to the ox:*
Everyone knows his own affairs.

affruntu *n.m.* affront, shame.
A tavula nun cci voli affruntu. Source: Pitrè, IV, 82.
Eng. *At the dinner table there is no need to be ashamed or embarassed.*

aggenti *n.f.* people, crowd, acquaintances.
Cu' havi argentu, havi aggenti. Source: Pitrè, III, 256.
Eng. *Whoever has money, has agents.*

agghiùttiri *v.t.* swallow.
Pigghiati chiddu morsu chi pò agghiuttiri.. Source: Pitrè, IV, 128.
Eng. *Don't bite off more than you can chew.*

Lit. Take the morsel you can swallow.

aggravari *v.t.* to worsen, aggravate.
Quannu lu zitu nun voli la zita, s'aggrava a la doti.
Eng. When a groom does not want to marry the bride to be, he finds fault with the dowry.

Agustinu *n.m.* Augustine.
Nun cc' è tavula senza vinu,
Nè predica senza Agustinu. Source: Pitrè, IV, 141.
Eng. A table is not complete without wine.
Nor a sermon without Augustine.

alcunu *pron., adj.* somebody, someone, anybody, anyone. *Also: caccunu, quarcunu.*
Alcuni su' ancili 'n chiesa e diavuli 'n casa. Source: Pitrè, IV, 64.
Eng. Some are angels in church and devils at home.

ali *n.f.* wings, dice.
Li dinari hannu l'ali. Source: Pitrè, III, 264.
Eng. Money has wings.

allattatu *n.f.* whitened.
Muru allattatu è carta di mbriàchi. Source: Piccitto, II, 911.
Eng. A blank wall invites graffiti.
Lit. A whitewashed wall is paper for drunkards.

allittiratu *adj.* educated, learned.
Libbru sirratu nun fa l'omu littiratu. Source: Pitrè, III, 203.
Eng. A closed book does not make an educated man.
Pitrè quotes Goethe: "How many are those who think they are learned for having a good number of books on their shelves; or for having read and memorized many title pages!"

allura *adv.* then, in that case.
Li cosi 'un vennu allura. Source: Pitrè, IV, 17.
Eng. The causes of inflictions are not always recognized.
Tr. note: Pitrè explains that *Li cosi* refers to hurts or infirmities, which often times are not connected back to their causes.

aluzzu *n.m.* zool. pike.

Cuda d'aluzzu e testa d'ariccìola. Source: Pitrè, IV, 86.
Eng. *The tail of the pike and the head of the leerfish are good to eat.*

amari *v.t.* to love, to prefer.
Amari e disamari nun sta a cui lu voli fari. Source: Pitrè, I, 101.
Eng. *You don't choose whom to love and not love.*

ammuccia *v.t.* hides, conceals.
Cu' ammuccia zoccu fa,
È signu chi mali fa. Source: Pitrè, III, 301.
Eng. *A secretive person*
Is up to no good.

amuri *n.m.* love.
Amuri nun senti cunsigghi. Source: Pitrè, I, 105.
Eng. *Love doesn't listen to advice.*

Amuri, tussi e fumu nun si ponnu tèniri cilati. Source: Pitrè, I, 106.
Eng. *Love, coughing, and smoke can't be kept concealed.*

Amuri, tutti dìcinu ch'è amaru, e ognunu voli pruvari siddu è veru.
Eng. *Love, everyone says it's bitter, but everyone wants to see for himself*
if it's true.

Benchì l'amuri novu trova locu, scurdari nun si pò l'amuri anticu.
Eng. *Although there's a new love, the old love can't be forgotten.*

Juramenti d'amuri e fumu di ciminia,
L'acqua li lava e lu ventu si li carrìa. Source: Pitrè, IV, 215.
Eng. *Promises of love, and chimney smoke,*
Are washed away by water and blown away by wind.

Tantu si trova amuri sutta lana quantu sutta sita. Source: Pitrè, I, 119;
Eng. *Wealth is not what makes gentility.*
Lit. *As much love is found under wool as under silk.*

anca *n.f.* hip, side, thigh, leg.
Addùmamu la lampa,
E poi mànciamu l'anca. (***Palermo***). Source: Pitrè, II, 20.
Eng. *Let's light the lamp*

19

And then we'll eat the leg of lamb.
Tr. note: This saying comes from the practice of the friars or hermits who would first pay homage to the various saints and then rekindle the lamps for each of them. They would eat after having thus fulfilled their obligation.

ancèlicu *adj.* angelic.
Lu farfanti voli aviri la menti ancèlica. Source: Pitrè, IV, 60.
Eng. *The rogue wants to have an angelic mind.*

ancilina *adv. loc.* left fallen.
L'oliva lassata all'ancilina, nun jinchi nè visazza nè sacchettina. Source: Pitrè, IV, 379.
Eng. *Uncollected olives, left to the elements, fill neither the saddle bag nor the waist pack.*

aneddu *n.m.* ring, band, teething ring, bot. tendril, ringlet, lock, curl.
La vuccuzza è comu 'n aneddu
Si mancia turri, palazzu e casteddu. Source: Pitrè, IV, 94.
Eng. *The little mouth is like a ring*
Yet it consumes towers, palaces and castles.

annigarisi *v.tr.* to drown.
Annigarisi 'nt' on gottu d'acqua. Source: Traina, 444.
Eng. *To perish over a trifle.*
Lit. *To drown in a mug of water.*

annittari *v.t.* to clean, purge, empty, sift, winnow.
Quannu unu nesci di lu fangu, s' annetta li scarpi. Source: Pitrè, IV, 175.
Eng. *When someone steps out of the mud, he cleans off his shoes.*
Pitrè notes: "That's how it is after having had dealings with people who are dishonest, depressing and wicked."

annu *n.m.* year.
Anni e piccati su' cchiù di quantu si dicinu. Source: Bellantonio, II, 208.
Eng. *Age and peccadillos are usually more than stated.*

Pani d'un jornu e vinu d'un annu. Source: Pitrè, IV, 103.
Eng. *Eat today's bread and last year's wine.*

antimòniu *n.m.* dampness of the sulphur mine.
Quattru sunnu li nnimici di l' omu: Dimoniu, antimoniu, matrimoniu e

Tribunali di Patrimoniu. Source: Pitrè, IV, 190.
Eng. *Four are the scourges of man: the Devil, the dampness of the sulphur mine, matrimony, and the probate court.*

antividiri *v.t.* foresee, predict.
Si campari vôi sicuru, antividi lu futuru. Source: Pitrè, III, 369.
Eng. *If you want to live secure foresee the future.*

apprenniri *v.t.* learn, understand; ignite.
Cui sta a mastru e nun apprenni, o è asinu o si finci. Source: Pitrè, II 178.
Eng. *He who is an apprentice and does not learn is either a jackass or pretends he is one.*

archeologgia *n.f.* Archaeology.
Solunto, situated on the north coast in the province of Palermo close to Bagheria, is one of the ancient settlements of the Phoenicians. The illustration depicts the ruins of the peristyle that has become an icon of the site.

arma, *n.f.* **armu** *n.m.* soul, spirit, sensitivity, heart.
L'armu cc' è, li forzi no. Source: Alaimo, 154.
Eng. *The spirit is willing but the flesh is weak.*

L'arma di l'omu è lu ciatu di Diu. Source: Pitrè, III, 342.
Eng. *God's breath is man's soul.*
Tr. note: This proverb is in Pitrè, Volume III, Chapter 72, Religion.

arricogghiri *v.t.* harvest, reap, pick up, collect, gather, envelop, receive.
Zoccu si simina s'arricogghi. Source: Traina, 79.
Eng. *Whatever one sows, that will he also reap.*

asciutto *v.t.* dry.
Asciutti li pedi, càuda la testa,
E di lu restu campa di bestia. Source: Pitrè, IV, 5.
Eng. *Keep your feet dry and your head warm,*
For the rest live as a beast.

aspittari *v.t.* await, expect.
Cu' havi tempu, nun aspittassi tempu. Source: Pitrè, III, 373.
Eng. *Don't waste your time.*

L'acqua e la morti, aspettala ca veni. Source: Pitrè, III, 104, and Zinna, 118.
Eng. *Nothing is certain but death and taxes.*
Lit. *Rain and death, wait, for they will come.*

avviniri *n.m.* time to come, future.
Voi ca ti 'mbizzi a nun falliri?
Pensa a lu passatu e all'avviniri. Source: Pitrè, III, 370.
Eng. *Do you want to learn how not to fail?*
Think of the past and the future.

avvizzari *v.t.* accustom, adapt.
Gatta avvizzata a manciari saimi,
Sempri la trovi allatu lu muzzuni. Source: Pitrè, IV, 152.
Eng. *The cat accustomed to eating lard,*
Is always found next to the clay pot.
Tr. note: Damaged clay pots (**muzzuni**), no longer useful for their primary purpose, depending on their size, were used to hold salt, flour, lard, and other foodstuffs that could be stored for future use.

azioni *n.f.* acts, action.
Ognunu è figghiu di l'azioni soi. Source: Pitrè, I, 346
Eng. *Everyone is responsible for his own acts.*

azzalori *n.f.pl. bot.* loquat, medlar.
Li cutugna pri l'èrrami ziti,
L'azzalori (nèspuli) pri l'omini boni. Source: Pitrè, IV, 95.
Eng. *The quince is for quarrelsome fiancées,*
The loquats for good folks.
Pitrè adds: La cotogna è segno di dispetto, o di cordoglio per le spose.
Eng. For brides the quince is a sign of spite or grief.

babbanu *adj.* foolish, stupid.
Nun cc' è peju d'aviri a fari cu babbani. Source: Pitrè, IV, 45.
Eng. *There's nothing worse than having to deal with fools.*

Si lu riccu nun fussi babbanu,
Nun purria campari lu viddanu. Source: Pitrè, III, 276.
Eng. *Were the rich man not stupid,*
The peasant would not be able to survive.

baccalaru *n.m.* codfish, fool, tardy person, female genitalia, crude error,
syphilis.
Corpu di baccalaru arrassu sia. Source: Pitrè, IV, 7.
Eng. *May heaven protect you from the French sickness.*
Pitrè notes: Il cielo ti guardi da mal francese.
Eng. May heaven protect you from the French sickness.

badagghiu *n.m.* yawn.
Lu bàdagghiu 'un pò mintiri:
O voli manciari, o voli durmiri. Source: Pitrè, IV, 19.
Eng. *The yawn doesn't lie:*
It wants you to eat or sleep.

Bagaria *n.f.* Bagheria.
Acqua a la Bagaria, ventu a li Coddi e furtuna di mari a li Ciacuddi. Source:
Pitrè, III, 130.
Eng. *Water at Bagheria, wind at Coddi and gifts of the sea at Ciacuddi.*
Tr. note: Pitrè says that these are the things that are lacking or extremely rare
in the three locations. The proverb is in Pitrè, Volume III, Chapter 60, Peoples,
Countries, Cities.

bagascia *n.f.* harlot, whore, hooker.
Sbirri, bagasci e cani, quannu su' vecchi morinu di fami.
Eng. *Cops, hookers, and dogs, when they're old they die of hunger.*

bagghiu *n.m.* courtyard.
Nun su' boni du' gaddi 'ntra un bagghiu. Source: Pitrè, I, 84.
Eng. *It's not a good idea to have two roosters in the same courtyard.*

balata *n.f.* slate, flagstone, stone tomb cover.
Camurria 'nvicchiata, ti lassa a la balata. Source: Pitrè, IV, 6.
Eng. *You'll be rid of chronic gonorrhea at your tomb.*
Tr. note: That was the outlook until the 20th century.

balataru *n.m.* palate, fig. taste. Also: **balatu, palataru.**
A cui havi guastu lu balataru
Ogni cibbu cci pari amaru. Source: Pitrè, I, 11.
Eng. *To someone with a damaged palate*
All foods seem bitter.

ballu *n.m.* dance, ball.
Mentri semu 'ntra lu ballu cci abballamu. Source: Pitrè, III, 384.
Eng. *When in Rome do as the Romans.*
Lit. *While we're at the ball, we'll dance.*

banna *n.f.* side, part, place.

A banna unni si' 'nvitatu, vacci. Source: Pitrè, III, 312.
Eng. *Go wherever you're invited.*

Lu bonu gaddu canta a tutti banni. Source: Pitrè, II 15.
Eng. *A good rooster crows everywhere.*
Unu senza vizzii a tutti banni va. Source: Pitrè, IV, 155.
Eng. *A man without vices fits everywhere.*

bannera *n.f.* banner.
La donna teni quattru banneri:
Càrzara, malatia, furca e galeri. Source: Pitrè, IV, 231.
Lit. *The woman holds four banners:*
Jail, sickness, the gallows, and prisons.

baratteri *n.m.* discounter, barterer.
La puvirtà fa l'omu baratteri. Source: Pitrè, III, 262.
Eng. *Poverty makes a man a discounter.*

Bartulumeu *n.m.* Bartholomew
Cu havi un pedi a lu burdellu, nn'havi n'àutru a San Bartulumeu. Source:
Pitrè, IV, 150.
Eng. *He who frequents the brothel will soon end up at Saint Bartholomew's.*
Tr. note: San Bartulumeu was a hospital for incurables dedicated to the care of
those suffering with syphilis. It then became S. Spirito, a hospice for the homeless.

Nè di casu varca, nè di pani Bartulumeu. Source: Pitrè, IV, 102.
Eng. *Don't dig out the insides of the cheese, nor peel the crust off the*
bread.
Tr. note: This proverb refers to Saint Bartholomew about whom little is known.
According to tradition, he was martyred by being skinned alive.

basta *adv,* enough, sufficiently.
Nun è picca mai chiddu chi basta. Source: Pitrè, IV, 125.
Eng. *That which is enough is never too little.*

Bastianu *n.m.* Sebastian.
A lu jornu di San Bastianu,
La nivi chianu chianu (**Chiaramonte**). Source: Pitrè, III, 10.
Eng. *On St. Sebastian's Day,*
The snow covers everything.
Tr. note: The festival day for St. Sebastian is January 20.

batia *n.f.* abbey, monastery, orphanage, pear variety.
Batii e spiziarii, pri sapiri li fatti di l'autri. Source: Pitrè, IV, 376.
Eng. *Go to abbeys and pharmacies, to know everyone else's business.*

Prima d' 'a pulizia
Si sapi n' 'a batia (***Chiaramonte***). Source: Pitrè, IV, 376.
Eng. *It's known in the abbey*
Before it's known by the police.

battagghiu *n.m.* clapper.
Dissi la campana a lu battagghiu,
Ogni cosa ch'arresta è pri lu megghiu. Source: Pitrè, III, 248.
Eng. *Said the bell to its clapper,*
Everything that stops is for the better.
Tr. note: This proverb is in Pitrè, Volume III, Chapter 66, Patience, Resignation.

battiri *v.t.* strike, beat, knock, touch.
Batti lu ferru mentri è càudu. Source: Pitrè, III, 383.
Eng. *Strike while the iron is hot.*

Va pri la strata battuta. Source: Pitrè, IV, 178.
Eng. *Take the road well traveled.*
Tr. note: Rather than Robert Frost's, The Road Not Taken.

"...I shall be telling this with a sigh
Somewhere ages and ages hence:
Two roads diverged in a wood, and I,
I took the one less traveled by,
And that has made all the difference."

bbicchibbacchi *n.m.* narrow necked jug or pitcher.
Ti scanti di lu bicchi-bacchi,
E di lu tira-stocchi no? Source: Pitrè, IV, 72.
Eng. *Having a groundless fear.*
Lit. *Fearing the narrow necked jug,*
And not the extraction?
Tr. note: This may be a reference to the narrow necked jug, also called a bummulu which was used to administer liquid medications or herbal remedies that the pharmacist compounded for the patient.
Tr. note: Piccitto gives the spelling as **bbicchibbacchi.**

beccu *n.m.* spout, beak; male goat.

È fattu lu beccu a l'oca. Source: Traina, 117.
Eng. *All's well that ends well.*
Lit. The beak of the goose is made.

beni *n.m.* good, means, property.
Beni di furtuna pàssanu comu la luna.
Eng. *Easy come, easy go.*

Cui fa beni pr'amuri,
S'acquista la grazia di lu Signuri. Source: Pitrè, III, 121.
Eng. *He who does good out of love*
Gains the blessing of the Lord.

Fa beni e scordatillu, fa mali e pènsaci. Source: Pitrè, I, 184.
Eng. *Do good and forget it; do bad and reflect on it.*

Quannu lu poviru veni a beni, nun c'è terra chi lu teni.
Eng. *When a poor man gets lucky, nothing can contain him.*

Tinta dda casa unni 'un trasi beni. Source: Pitrè, III, 253.
Eng. *Sorry the house that lacks necessities.*

biancu *adj.* white, agr. barren.
Terra niura, duna bonu pani; terra bianca, prestu stanca. Source: Pitrè, I, 67.
Eng. *Fertile soil gives good bread; barren soil is quickly exhausted.*

biasimari *v.t.* disparage, belittle, degrade, blame.
Nuddu divi biasimari l'arti chi nun sapi.. Source: Bellantonio, II 130.
Eng. *No one should belittle skills he does not have.*

biatu *adj.* blessed, blest, happy. Also: **miatu**.
Biatu cui mori a lettu! Source: Pitrè, IV, 258.
Eng. *Blessed is the one who dies in bed!*

Biata dda casa ch'havi 'na cricchia rasa.
Eng. *Blessed is the house that has a son who is a cleric.*

biccheri *n.m.* water glass.
C' un bicchieri di vinu si fa un amicu. Source: Pitrè, IV, 137.

Eng. With a glass of wine you make a friend.

biddizza *n.f.* beauty.
Biddizza e crianza raru si ponnu aviri. Source: Pitrè, 1, 161.
Eng. You rarely see both beauty and good manners.

billi-billi *n.f.pl.* sweet-talk.
Nun tantu billi billi, ch'un sulu billi basta. Source: Pitrè, IV, 127.
Eng. Just a little sweet-talk will do.

binchì *conj.* although, however.
Binchì nun parri, la facci t'accusa. Source: Pitrè, IV, 65.
Eng. Though you say nothing, your face accuses you.
Tr. note: Attempting to divine someone's thoughts by the look on their face can be very misleading.

birrutu *adj.* testy, petulant, peevish, cantankerous.
Diu vi scanza d'omu birrutu e di fimmina macadura. Source: Pitrè, IV, 230.
Eng. May God spare you from a peevish man and a lazy woman.

buffa *n.f.* toad.
Quannu chiovi e fa lu scuru
Megghiu buffa di margiu chi vujaru. Source: Pitrè, III, 53.
Eng. When it's raining and dark
It's better to be a swamp toad than a cowherd.

cacaniru *n.m.* last born, smartest. Also: **cacanidu**.
Lu cacaniru si cugghìu tutti li sbièzzii. Source: Bellantonio, II 155.
Eng. The last born is the smartest.
Lit. The last born took all the pepper.

caccia *n.f.* hunt, chase, catch.
Quannu la caccia nun ti dici, vattinni ad accampari babbaluci. Source: Pitrè, III, 249.
Eng. When the hunt is not successful, go harvest snails.

Quannu tu vidi ca la caccia 'un dici,
Càlati 'n terra e cogghi babbaluci. Source: Pitrè, III, 249.
Eng. When you see that the hunt is not successful,

Bend down and harvest snails.

cacciaturi *n.m.* hunter.
Lu cani cacciaturi, quannu abbaja è signu chi la caccia havi vicina. Source: Pitrè, 1, 132.
Eng. *When the hunting dog barks, it's a signal that the prey is near.*

L'omu è cacciaturi. Source: Pitrè, II, 99.
Eng. *Man is a hunter.*
Pitrè adds: "And however he can allow himself to make love with this or this other woman. The proverb is used on purpose to excuse the actions and escapades of those who meet their obligations less than do honest and faithful husbands."

caciu *n.m.* cheese.
Nè di caciu varca, nè di pani Bartulumeu.
Eng. *It's not polite to eat just the center of the cheese and just the crust of the bread.*

cacòcciula *n.f.* artichoke.
Sintirisi cacòcciula.
Eng. *To feel too proud and self-centered.*

caciuni *n.f.* cause, fault, occasion.
Morti nun veni mai senza caciuni. Source: Pitrè, IV, 256.
Eng. Death never comes without cause.
Tr. note: Also **scaciuni** and **accaciuni.**

caddusi *adj.* calloused, hardened.
Manu caddusi, manu gluriusi. Source: Pitrè, III, 188.
Eng. Calloused hands are glorious hands.

cadiri *v.i.* fall, happen, succeed.
Arvulu forti prestu cadi. Source: Pitrè, IV, 114.
Eng. The bigger they are, the harder they fall.
Lit. A strong tree falls quickly.

'Mbriàcati di vinu bonu e lassa ca cadi. Source: Pitrè, IV, 141.
Eng. Get drunk with good wine. come what may.

Si ti sonni chi cadi, cùrriti a sagnari. Source: Pitrè, IV, 30.
Eng. If you dream that you're falling, cure yourself with a bloodletting.

caduta *n.f.* fall, fallen, sunset, waterfall, skirt, drip, fish net.
Anciddi di caduta sunnu rari. Source: Pitrè, IV, 82.
Eng. Eels are rarely caught with a net.

Cui casca e si spingi, nun si chiama caduta. Source: Pitrè, IV, 145.
Eng. When someone falls and gets up. his cannot be called a fall.
cafè *n.m.* coffee.

Lu cafè santiannu e lu cicculatti ripusannu.
Eng. Drink coffee while it's hot enough to make you swear but let the hot chocolate cool.

caiccu *n.m.* caique, boat, craft, skiff.
Cc' è sempri lu locu pi lu caiccu (**Palermo**). Source: Pitrè, IV, 85.
Eng. There's always room for a skiff.
Pitrè explains: "Significa: malgrado che si sia mangiato, non si è poi tanto sazi che all' occasione non si possa prendere ancora un boccone. Questo proverbio corre tra la gente di mare." It means: Even though someone has eaten, they're not so sated that, on occasion they can't take another mouthful. This proverb is current among seamen.

calamità *n.f.* calamity, misfortune. *Also:* **calamitati**.
'Ntra tempi filici, si trovanu amici;
'Ntra li calamitati, nun vi spianu comu stati. Source: Pitrè, III, 252.
Eng. *In good times, you find friends;*
In calamitous times, they don't ask how you are.

càlia *n.f.* roasted chick peas.
Sosizza di Mazzarinu, càlia di Cartagiruni e pasta di Vizzini.
Eng. *Sausage from Mazzarino, roasted chick peas from Caltagirone, and pasta from Vizzini.*

calici *n.m.* chalice.
Lu parrinu cummogghia lu calici e nui nn'avemu a cummigghiari l'unu cu l'àutru.
Eng. *The priest covers the chalice and we must cover each other.*

camina *v.t.* walks.
La donna e la gaddina si perdi si troppu camina.
Eng. *The woman, like the hen, gets lost if she walks too far.*

Omu senza dinari, è mortu chi camina. Source: Pitrè, III, 273.
Eng. *A man without money is a dead man walking.*

caminu *n.m.* road, travel, way.
Nun ti mettiri 'n caminu
Si la tò vucca nun sapi di vinu. Source: Pitrè, IV, 26.
Eng. *Don't set off*
Before you've tasted the wine.

Ogni migghiu di caminu havi un pezzu di malu caminu. Source: Pitrè, III, 93.
Eng. *There's a rough patch along every mile of road.*

càmmara *n.f.* room, bedroom, chamber.
Putirisi cociri l'ova 'nta 'na càmmara. Source: Traina, 144.
Eng. *It's so hot, you could cook an egg in the room.*

campa *v.i. 3rd p.sing.* lives.
Cui cchiù campa, cchiù 'mpinatisci.
Eng. *The longer you live the more you suffer.*

campagna *n.f.* countryside.
Di campagna veni lu beni (***Ficarazzi***). Source: Pitrè, I, 55.
Eng. *Good things come from the countryside.*

campana *n.f.* bell.
A lu sonu si conusci la campana. Source: Pitrè, III, 300.
Eng. *You know the bell by its sound.*

campari *v.i.* to live, to be alive.
Cchiù si campa cchiù si 'mpara. Source: Pitrè, II 174.
Eng. *The longer you live the more you learn.*

Si mancia pri campari, nun si campa pri manciari.
Eng. *Eat to live, not live to eat.*

Vôi campari? lassa campari.
Eng. *Live and let live.*
Lit. *Do you want to live? Let live.*

campavita *n.f.* making a living.
La campavita è cchiù forti di li peni di lu 'nfernu (***Marsala***). Source: Pitrè,
Vol IV, page 260.
Eng. *Making a living is hard as hell.*
Lit. *Making a living is harder than the pains of hell.*

càncari *n.m.* cancers, troubles, hinges.
Lassatimi stari pri li càncari mei.
Eng. *Let me deal with my troubles myself.*

cància *v.t.* changes, trades, barters, transforms, alters.
Cui cancia, si leva li crozzi e tinci.
Eng. *Whoever changes gets rid of the coarse and the bad.*

Fimmina e ventu, cància ogni mumentu.
Eng. *A woman and the wind change every moment.*

Nun si cància la facci pri dinari. Source: Pitrè, III, 284.
Eng. *Don't compromise your beliefs for money.*

cani *n.m.* dog.

Acqua e pani, vita di cani. Source: Pitrè, IV, 80.
Eng. *Bread and water, a dog's life.*

Nun tràsiri cani dintra, cà ti pòrtanu l'ossa fora. Source: Pitrè, IV, 173.
Eng. *Beware of false friends with wagging tongues.*
Lit. *Don't bring dogs inside because they'll take your bones outside.*

Varda lu cani pri rispettu di lu patruni. Source: Zinna, 125.
Eng. *Love me, love my dog.*
Lit. *Look kindly on the dog out of respect for its owner.*

canigghia *n.f.* skin, peel, grain chaff.
Sparagnari la canigghia e sfragari la farina. Source: Traina, 150.
Eng. *Penny wise and pound foolish.*
Lit. *Sparing the chaff and squandering the flour.*

canna *n.f.* cane, stick, fish rod, ancient measure 2.08 M, grain stalk, any tube such as a rifle barrel, boot legging.
Canna torta, pisci porta. Source: Pitrè, III, 301.
Eng. *A bent rod catches a fish.*

cannarozzu *n.m.* esophagus, throat.
Si ti sonni ca ti dolinu li cannarozza, lèvati sangu. Source: Pitrè, IV, 30.
Eng. *If you dream that your throat hurts, have a bleeding done.*

cannata *n.f.* jug, pitcher, mug.
Lu piattu e la cannata,
Fannu la facci 'ncarnata. Source: Pitrè, IV, 98.
Eng. *The dish and the jug,*
Make the face redden.

cannila *n.f.* candle, oil lamp, jest. snot, small pipe.
Guai a cu' è riduttu a la cannila. Source: Pitrè, III, 261.
Eng. *Wretched is the man who is in the throes of death.*

Ogni santu voli la sò cannila. Source: Pitrè, I, 10.
Eng. *Every saint deserves his own candle.*

Cannilora *n.f.* Candlemas.
A la Cannilora (2 febb.) di lu 'nvernu semu fora. Source: Pitrè, III, 6.
Eng. *By Candlemas we are done with winter.*

A la Cannilora,
Ogni gaddina veni ad ova. Source: Pitrè, III, 8.
Eng. *At the time of Candlemas,*
Every hen will lay.

cannolu *n.m.* hair roller, tube.
Ammatula t'allisci e fa' cannola:
Bedda cci vô' viniri di natura. Source: Pitrè, 1, 161.
Eng. *It's useless to doll up and act seductively*
Beauty is endowed by nature.

cantu *n.m.* corner.
San Simuni, acqua pro li vadduni,
Tutti i Santi, nivi pri li canti. Source: Pitrè, I, 31.
Eng. *By St. Simon (Oct. 28), water in the ravines.*
By All Saints, snow on the street corners.

cantunera *n.f.* cornerstone, corner, corner of a room, street corner, pillar.
Sugnu misu 'nta sta cantunera
Guardami cui sugnu e no cu' era. Source: Pitrè, III, 304.
Eng. *I've been pigeonholed*
Look at me as I am and not as I was.

canusciri *v.t.* know, recognize, understand, realize.
Lu minchiuni 'un si conusci quannu nasci;
Si conusci quannu crisci. Source: Pitrè, IV, 43.
Eng. *A fool is not recognized when he's born;*
He's recognized when he grows up.

capiddu *n.m.* hair.
La furtuna si pigghia pri li capiddi. Source: Pitrè, III, 378.
Eng. *Grab luck by the hair.*

Tira cchiù un capiddu di fimmina chi 'na corda di bastimentu. Source: Pitrè, I, 119.
Eng. *One strand of a woman's hair pulls more than a ship's hawser.*

capitari *v.t.* occur, happen, be caught, win.
Si pigghia la cosa quannu càpita. Source: Pitrè, I, 324.
Eng. *When opportunity knocks, open the door.*

cappeddu *n.m.* hat, fig. man.
Quantu va un cappeddu
'Un cci vannu centu fodeddi. Source: Pitrè, IV, 223.
Lit. The worth of one hat
Is not equalled by a hundred skirts.
Tr. note: hat refers to a professional person and skirts refers to houswives.

carbuni. *n.m.* coal. Also: **carvuni, carvunu.**
Amicu chi finci, è comu lu carvuni; o t' ardi o tinci. Source: Pitrè, IV, 64.
Eng. The friend who pretends, is like coal; it either burns you or blackens
you.

carnalmenti *adv.* by the flesh, carnally.
Cui vivi carnalmenti, nun dura lungamenti. Source: Pitrè, IV, 151.
Eng. He who lives by the flesh, does not live long.
Pitrè adds the note: "I never heard this said, but I find it in various manuscripts of the past century."

carnilivari *n.m.* carnival, Mardi gras, Shrove Tuesday.
Lu Carnilivari mancia cu cu' voi,
E La Pasqua mangia cu li toi. Source: Pitrè, III, 48.
Eng. During Carnival eat with whomever you want,
And celebrate Easter with your family.

carpistari *v.t.* trample, tread, stand on.
Avemu bisognu di la terra chi carpistamu. Source: Pitrè, IV, 179.
Eng. We have need of the land we tread upon.

carricari *v.t.* load down, carry, load a pistol, reinvigorate oneself, charge, invoice.
Megghiu nasciri patedda 'ntra lu mari, ca sceccu a carricari.
Eng. Better to be born a limpet in the sea than a load bearing donkey.

carrozza *n.f.* carriage.
Lu cummannari è megghiu di jiri 'n carrozza. Source: Pitrè, I, 84.
Eng. Being in command is better than riding in the carriage.

carta *n.f.* paper, wallpaper, document, certificate, coupon, playing card.
Li picciriddi su' carta bianca. Source: Pitrè, II, 216.
Eng. Little children are a blank slate.
Lit: Little children are white paper.

Nè occhi 'n carta, nè manu 'n càscia. Source: Pitrè, III, 326.
Eng. *Neither peeking, nor stealing.*

carteddi *n.m.* baskets.
Cui fa carteddi, nni fa làidi e nni fa beddi. Source: Alaimo, 7.
Eng. *Basket makers, make some ugly and some beautiful.*

cartilèggii *n.f.* collected papers, notebook.
Quannu l'omu veni 'n puvirtati,
Cerca li cartilèggii di sò nannu. Source: Pitrè, III, 274.
Eng. *When a man is reduced to poverty.*
He searches through the papers of his grandfather (for some overlooked value).

carusu *n.m.* boy, apprentice, moneybox.
Conza la tavula e manna lu carusu all'acqua. Source: Pitrè, IV, 86.
Eng. *Set the table and send the boy for water.*

càrzari *n.m.* jail, prison. Also: **càrcira, càrzara, càrziri.**
Càrzari e malatìi, libbiràtinni miu Diu! Source: Pitrè, IV, 11.
Eng. *O Lord, deliver us from jails and illnesses.*

càscia *n.f.* trunk, chest, treasure chest, case, container, cash draw.
Nun cc' è casa senza càscia,
Nè casatu senza bagascia. Source: Pitrè, IV, 232.
Eng. *There isn't a house without a trunk.*
Nor an ancestry without a harlot.
Pitrè says this is a proverb of despair.

cassari *v.t.* cancel, break.
Ti vôi insignari a cassari cuntratti?
Simina òriu, e chianta catarrati (**Salaparuta**). Source: Pitrè, I, 70.
Eng. *Do you want to know how to earn enough to pay off your contracts?*
Sow barley and plant catarrati type grapes.
Tr. note: Pitrè adds that the catarrati grape has an abundant production.

cassata *n.f.* cassata, dessert made with ricotta.
Tintu cu' 'un mancia cassati la matina di Pasqua. Source: Pitrè, III, 277.
Eng. *Pity those who don't eat cassata on Easter morning.*
Note by Pitrè: **Cassata,** the sweet cake found all over Sicily, is especially eaten on Easter which is therefore called Easter of the cassati to distinguish if from Easter

of the flowers, which is Pentecost.

castagna *n.f.* chestnut, chestnut tree.
Castagni, olivi e ghianna, Agustu nn'addimanna. Source: Pitrè, I, 46.
Eng. Chestnuts, olives, and acorns, ask for them in August.
castigari *v.t.* castigate, chastise, chasten, reprove.

Quannu Diu voli castigari all'omu, cci leva lu lumi. Source: Pitrè, I, 347.
Eng. When God wants to chastise man, He takes away his lamp (good sense).

catina *n.f.* chain, bond, leash, tie, mountain range.
Catinazzu 'mmucca. Source: Pitrè, III, 216.
Eng. Zip your lip.

cattiva *n.f.* widow.
Lu granu di la cattiva va alla chiazza e torna e riggira.
Eng. The widow's two cents go to the plaza and turn and come back.
Tr. note: She's not spending carelessly.

catu *n.m.* pail, bucket.
Si iunciu 'u catu câ corda.
Eng. Together like two peas in a pod.
Lit. Joined like the bucket and the rope.

càudu *adj.* hot, warm.
Batti lu ferru mentri è càudu.
Eng. Strike while the iron is hot.

Quannu in sittembri càuru e asciuttu domina,
La terra si pripara pri la sèmina. Source: Pitrè, I, 59.
Eng. When hot and dry weather dominates in September,
It's time to prepare the soil for seeding.
Tr. note: Mina Palumbo says this proverb fits well for the farms at higher elevations like the Petralie.

cavaddu *n.m.* horse.
A cavaddu d' àutru 'un circari sedda. Source: Pitrè, III, 313.
Eng. Look after your own affairs.
Lit. Don't look for a saddle for someone else's horse.

cavari *v.t.* dig, excavate, extract.
Pani cu l' occhi, furmaggiu senz' occhi e vinu chi ti cava l' occhi. Source: Pitrè, IV, 104.
Eng. *Bread with eyes, cheese without eyes, and wine that pulls your eyes out.*

caviali *n.m.* capital, investment, pretext, excuse.
Ad essiri asinu 'un cci voli caviali. Source: Pitrè, IV, 34.
Eng. *You don't need an excuse to be a jackass.*
Tr. note: This proverb is in Pitrè, Volume IV, Chapter 76, Knowledge, Ignorance.

celu *n.m.* sky, paradise, heaven.
Tutti semu sutta lu celu. Source: Pitrè, III, 99.
Eng. *We're all under the same sky.*

centu *n.m.* one hundred.
Cu' fa centu e nun fa l'unu, perdi lu centu pri causa di l'unu.
Eng. *Finish what you start.*
Lit. He who makes the hundred and not the one, loses the hundred because of the one.

cera *n.f.* facial aspect, look, appearance, mien.
Cani chi fa cera a tanti nun havi patruni. Source: Pitrè, IV, 258.
Eng. *A dog that is friendly with many doesn't have an owner.*

cercari *v.t.* seek.
Cerca, ca trovi. Source: Pitrè, III, 193.
Eng. *Seek and ye shall find.*

cerniri *v.t.* to sift, to sieve.
Cu ddu ventu chi mina cernu e spagghia.
Eng. *With the wind that blows, sifts and winnows.*

cèusi *n.m.* mulberry tree.
Cèusi e ficu, siacci nnimicu! Source: Pitrè, I, 34.
Eng. *Mulberry and fig trees should be pruned mercilessly!*
Lit. *Be the enemy of mulberry and fig trees!*

chianu *n.m.* plain, plaza, courtyard, floor of a building, deck of a ship, farmstead.

Quannu amuri è capitanu, la muntagna pari chianu. Source: Pitrè, IV, 216.
Eng. *Love conquers all.*
Lit. *When love is the guide, the mountain seems a plain.*

chiddu *pron.* that, who.
Chiddu chi nun è pò essiri. Source: Pitrè, IV, 180.
Eng. *Everything is possible.*
Lit. *That which is not, can be.*

Chiuppu *n.m.* Pioppo; poplar tree, Lat. populus dilatata.
Prima Diu e poi l'acqua di lu Chiuppu,
'N Palermu cci arrivanu chini a tappu. Source: Pitrè, II, 440.
Eng. *First God and then the water from Pioppo, In Palermo the barrels will arrive filled to the cork.*
Tr. note: On their trip transporting wine from Partinico to Palermo, the cart drivers would usually stop in the village of Pioppo (Chiuppu) to eat and drink handsomely; drawing wine from their cargo. They would then add Pioppo's water to each barrel, to make up for the wine they had consumed, arriving in Palermo with full barrels.

ciàula *n.f.* magpie.
Gattaredda di firraru e ciàula di campanaru. Source: Pitrè, I, 4.
Eng. *The blacksmith's cat and the bell ringer's magpie.*
Tr. note: Said of a person who doesn't get flustered.

cima *n.f.* summit, rod to measure cask contents.
Nun pigghiati li cimi di l'aria. Source: Pitrè, IV, 127.
Eng. *Don't blow your top.*

ciratu *n.m.* cold cream.
Lu ciratu tira e sana. Source: Pitrè, IV, 19.
Eng. *Cold cream pulls and heals.*
Tr. note: Pitrè adds, "It is said of **cerato di Galena** that is applied on sores."
Further note: In France it is known as **Cérat de Galien**. One of its formulations is documented in the French National Form Number 74. Galen was a Greek physician in the second century.

cirrichincì *n.m.* screech owl.
Accussì canta lu cirrincinciò:
Tintu patruni canciari si pò Source: Pitrè, I, 58.
Eng. *Thus sings the screech owl:*
A bad master can be changed.

Pitrè notes: "Chiò, assiuolo, cirrincinciò, stillozzo, e ghirlingò o zirlingi, uccelli che cantano nella primavera, in cui gli agricoltori sogliono sceglersi un padrone per l'anno colonico."

Eng. The chiò, horned owl, screech owl, stillozzo, and thrush or zirlingi, birds that sing in the springtime, when farm workers usually choose the boss they'll work for in the coming year.

Tr. note: The decision is not taken lightly because it could involve having to move an entire household.

còcciu *n.m.* harvest (Chiaramonte).
A tempu di còcciu, si dormi ccu 'n' occhiu (***Chiaramonte***). Source: Pitrè, IV, 211.
Eng. At harvest time you sleep with one eye open.

cogghiri *v.t.* gather, harvest, pick.
Cogghi 'ntra jornu lu meli e la cira,
E balla e joca 'ntra l' àira la sira. Source: Pitrè, I, 35.
Eng. Make hay while the sun shines.
Lit. Harvest honey and beeswax during the day.
Dance and play outside in the evening.

corna *n.m.* adultery, cuckold.
Unn' è monaci e parrini, cci su' corna e vastunati.
Eng. Where there are monks and priests, there is adultery and beatings.

cosa *n.f.* thing, matter, affair, business.
Di cosa veni cosa. Source: Pitrè, IV, 181.
Eng. One thing leads to another.

cridenza *n.f.* faith.
Cu' duna a cridenza (o fa cridenza) perdi l'amicu e perdi li dinari. Source: Traina, 237.
Eng. One who lends on faith, loses both his friend and his money.

cridiri *v.t.* believe, think, trust.
Cui cridi e cui nun cridi. Source: Pitrè, III, 121.
Eng. Some believe and some don't.

Li gatti si sèntinu, li cani si vìdinu e l'omini si crìdinu. Source: Pitrè, IV, 261.
Eng. Cats are heard, dogs are seen and men are believed.

cruci *n.f.* cross, sacrifice.
Cui nun ha cruci, nun è figghiu di Diu. Source: Pitrè, IV, 377.
Eng. He who bears no crosses, is not a son of God.

La cruci è fatta pri tutti. Source: Pitrè, IV, 379.
Eng. The cross is for everyone.

Nun c'è artari senza cruci. Source: Alaimo, 158.
Eng. There is no victory without sacrifice.
Lit. There is no altar without the cross.

cuda *n.f.* tail.
La testa a la padedda e la cuda a mari. Source: Pitrè, IV, 94.
Eng. Fish should be cooked while it's very fresh.
Lit. The head in the skillet and the tail (still) in the sea.

cunigghiu *n.m.* rabbit.
Quannu mai lu cunigghiu ha fattu ova? Source: Pitrè, III, 127.
Eng. You reap what you sow.
Lit. Since when has the rabbit laid eggs?

cunsigghi *n.m.* counsel, advice.
A bon cunsigghiu nun si trova prezzu. Source: Pitrè, I, 301.
Eng. Good advice is priceless.

Tutti su' boni a dari cunsigghi. Source: Pitrè, I, 284.
Eng. All are good at giving advice.

Un bon cunsigghiu nun si pò pagari. Source: Pitrè, I, 301.
Eng. Good advice is priceless.

Un bonu cunsigghiu va cchiù di li dinari. Source: Pitrè, I, 300.
Eng. A good piece of advice is worth more than money.

cuntu *n.m.* accounting, tale, narrative, reason.
Cu' scappa la cunta. Source: Pitrè, IV, 181.
Eng. He who escapes, recounts.
Tr. note: Like some of the holocaust survivors who were willing to recount the horror in order to bear witness.

Lu cuntu nun metti tempu. Source: Pitrè, IV, 182.
Eng. The narrative doesn't include the time.
Tr. note: From the fable, **Catherine The Learned**, found in Vol. I of Pitrè's collection of Sicilian fables. In the fable Catherine becomes pregnant. "The telling doesn't include the time", and after nine months she gives birth to a beautiful boy. Two similar proverbs are variations of this one.

Nun si pò dari cuntu a tutti. Source: Pitrè, IV, 171.
Eng. You can't satisfy everyone.

curti *n.f.* court, family and others of the ruler, residence of the ruler.
'N curti unni nun regna la virtuti, è un celu senza stiddi. Source: Pitrè, I, 85.
Eng. A court where virtue is missing is like a sky without stars.

cuscenza *n.f.* conscience, consciousness. Also: **cuscenzia, cuscienza**. La fami 'un havi cuscenza. Source: Pitrè, IV, 379.
Eng. Hunger has no conscience.

cuverna *n.m.* governs, rules.
La scienza è pazzia, si nun si cuverna cu lu bonu giudiziu. Source: Pitrè, IV, 41.

Eng. Knowledge is madness, if it's not governed by judgement.

detta *n.f.* debt
A setti, ti levi la detta;
A ottu, ti fa' lu cappottu. Source: Pitrè, I, 32.
Eng. When the harvest is seven times the seeding, with some difficulty, you pay off your debt.
When the harvest is eight times the seeding, you can also afford to dress yourself.
Tr. note: The English is a free translation of the interpretation of the proverb supplied to Pitrè by Prof. Raffaele Castelli.

diàvulu *n.m.* devil.

Quannu lu poviru duna a lu riccu, lu diàvulu si nni ridi. Source: Pitrè, III, 275.
Eng. *The devil laughs when the poor gives to the rich.*

difettu *n.m.* fault.
Li difetti di la zita s'ammùccianu cu la dota.
Eng. *The bride's faults are hidden by the dowry.*

Ogn'omu havi lu sò difettu.
Eng. *No one is perfect.*

dinari *n.m.* money, one of the suits of Sicilian playing cards.
Cu' havi dinari assai, sempri cunta. Source: Pitrè, III, 256.
Eng. *The person with a lot of money is always counting.*

discrizioni *n.f.* discretion, discernment, tact.
La discrizioni è matri d'ogni virtù. Source: Pitrè, IV, 121.
Eng. *Discretion is the mother of every virtue.*

disgrazia *n.f.* misfortune, mishap, disaster, disgrace.
Sfilànnusi la curuna, sfilanu li disgrazii. Source: Pitrè, III, 249.
Eng. *Revealing everything, revealing disgrace.*

dissapitu *adj.* insipid, mincing, without flavor.
Lu cocu si teni nni lu dissapitu (**Chiaramonti**). Source: Pitrè, IV, 96.
Eng. *A cook goes easy on the salt.*

domari *v.t.* tame.
Lu pisu doma la bestia. Source: Pitrè, III, 206.
Eng. *The burden tames the beast.*

donna *n.f.* woman.
La cchiù bona è china di lampi e trona. Source: Pitrè, IV, 231.
Eng. *The best woman is full of lightning and thunder.*

dormi *v.i.* sleeps.
Cani chi dormi, nun lu scuitari. Source: Alaimo, 5.
Eng. *Let a sleeping dog lie.*

drittu *n.m.* straight, right, honest, upright.

Cui va drittu, va afflittu. Source: Pitrè, I, 263.
Eng. *When you walk the straight and narrow, you get pebbles in your shoes.*

dumani *n.m.* tomorrow.
Zoccu pô' fari oggi, 'un lu fari dumani. Source: Pitrè, III, 389.
Eng. *Don't put off 'til tomorrow what you can do today.*

eccessu *n.m.* excess.
Ogni eccessu è viziu.
Eng. *Every excess is a vice.*

eredità *n.f.* inheritance.
La gaddina si spinna quannu è morta. Source: Traina, 423.
Eng. *Inheritance follows death.*
Lit. *A chicken is plucked when it's dead.*

erruri *n.m.* error, mistake.
L'erruri di li medici, tutti li cummogghia la terra.
Eng. *A doctor's mistakes all lie buried.*

erva *n.f.* grass, greenery, weeds..
Erva ch' 'un si conusci, nun si meti. Source: Pitrè, IV, 164.
Eng. *Don't harvest vegetation that you don't recognize.*

essiri *v.i.* be.
Èssiri non si pò cchiù di na vota. Source: Fulci, 136.
Eng. *You can't live more than once.*

està *n.f.* Summer.
Nun jinchi li visazzi està chi fa cucuzzi e ramurazzi.
Eng. *The summer that yields pumpkins and horseradishes won't fill us up.*

etisia *n.f.* med. consumption
Tri sunnu li rimèddii pri l'etisia di la vurza: cena di latti, pruvuli di granci e di giurani e limatura di corna di cervu. Source: Pitrè, III, 265.
Eng. *There are three remedies for consumption of the purse: a meal consisting of milk, dust of crabs and frogs, and filings of deer antler.*
Tr. note: The proverb is an example of the Sicilian sense of humor. For some serious Sicilian recipes refer to: *Cucina Paradiso: The Heavenly Food of Sicily*, by Clifford A. Wright, Simon & Schuster, New York, 1992.; and *Alla Tavola Di*

Nunzio Bruno: Con la cucina popolare Siciliana, by Corrado Di Pietro, Venilia Editrice, Montemerlo, 1994.

facci *n.f.* face.
Cui sputa 'n celu, 'n facci cci torna.
Eng. *Spit at the heavens and you'll get it back in your face.*

La facci è specchiu di l'omu. Source: Pitrè, IV, 219.
Eng. *The face is a window to the soul.*
Lit. *The face is a mirror of the man,*

La facci si vidi e no lu cori.Source: Pitrè, II 186.
Eng. *The face is seen and not the heart.*

factotum n.m. broker. Also: **fatturi, spidugghjafacenni, sensali, senzali.**
Lu sensali aggèvula tuttu.
Eng. *The broker facilitates all.*

fallutu *adj.* Bankrupt.
Mircanti fallutu è menzu arriccutu.
Eng. *The bankrupt merchant is half rich.*

fama *n.f.* good name, reputation.
Cui perdi la bona fama, perdi tuttu! Source: Pitrè, I, 206.
Eng. *Who loses his good name, loses everything.*

La fama vola. Source: Pitrè, I, 207.
Eng. *A good name is a sometime thing.*
Tr. Note: also in the sense that the word about someone gets around.

Mala fama, pruvidenza. Source: Pitrè, I, 209.
Eng. *Bad reputation, blame providence.*

fami *n.f.* hunger.
Nun cc' è megghiu sarsa di la fami. Source: Pitrè, IV, 92.
Eng. *There's no better sauce than hunger.*

famigghia *n.f.* family, household.
Famigghia assai, puvirtà vicina. Source: Pitrè, II 206.
Eng. *With a large family, poverty is close by.*

fattu *n.m.* Action, deed, event, business, affair.
Vali cchiù un fattu chi deci paroli. Source: Pitrè, II.
Eng. *Actions speak louder than words.*
Lit. *One deed is worth more than ten words.*

fava *n.f.* Fava bean, broad bean.
Cu 'na fava vò pigghiari du' gaddini? Source: Pitrè, IV, 259.
Eng. *Do you hope to get two chickens with a single fava?*

La navi camina e la fava si coci. Source: Pitrè, IV, 93.
Eng. *All's right with the world.*
Lit. *The ship travels and the fava cooks.*

ficudinnia *n.f.* Prickly pear. *Also: ficurinnia.*
Iri a guardari ficudinnia. Source: Traina, 379.
Eng. *Pass away.*

Cui nun si voli pùnciri, nun tuccassi ficudinnia. Source: Pitrè, I, 334.
Eng. *To not get pricked don't touch the prickly pear.*

Unni cc'è ficurinnia, cc'è cristiani (**Marsala**). Source: Pitrè, II, 447.
Eng. *Where there are prickly pears there are people.*

fidari *v.t.* trust, faith.
Nu nni putemu fidari mancu di ddu patri chi nni fici. Source: Pitrè, II 262.
Eng. *We can't even trust in the father that made us.*

finiri *v.t.* finish, end, stop.
Zoccu si cumincia, si finisci.

Eng. Finish what you start.

fogghiu *n.m.* leaf, page.
Assai fogghi e nenti frutti. Source: Pitrè, III, 280.
Eng. All appearance but no substance.
Lit. Lots of leaves but no fruit.

forza *n.f.* strength, force, power, might.
Forza di giuvini e cunsigghiu di vecchi. Source: Bellantonio, II, 211.
Eng. The strength of the young and the counsel of the old.

frummentu *n.m.* wheat.
Cui simìna pri Santa Lucia (*13 Dic.*),
Nun porta frummentu pri la via. Source: Pitrè, I, 40.
Eng. He who sows as late as St. Lucy's day,
Won't be carrying wheat to market.

frustari *v.t.* shame, hold up to contempt. Ognunu si frusta comu cci gusta.
Source: Pitrè, III, 126.
Eng. Everyone chooses his own poison.

Tutta la citati mi frustati,
Pri la mè casa nun mi passati. Source: Pitrè, IV, 263.
Eng. You shamed me with my neighbors,
By not stopping by, at my house.

fruttu *n.m.* fruit, income, gain, benefit.
Di lu fruttu si conusci l'arvulu. Source: Bellantonio, II 147 and Pitrè, III, 302.
Eng. From the fruit you will know the tree.

Unu si mancia la lumia, e a n'àutru cci allianu li denti. Source: Pitrè, I, 251.
Eng. Someone eats a sweet lemon, and someone else's teeth are set on edge.

fulmini *n.m.* lightning, thunder, fig. sudden disaster.
Jocu, focu; vinu, malu distinu; fimmini, fulmini. Source: Pitrè, IV, 378.
Eng. Gambling, fire; wine, bad destiny; women, lightning.

fùncia *n.f.* mushroom.
Funci e nidi, pigghiali comu li vidi. Source: Pitrè, IV, 90.
Eng. *Mushrooms and nests, pick them as you see them.*

gabbari *v.t.* fool, cheat, deceive.
'Na vota si gabba la vecchia; appressu vota vi chiuj la porta. Source: Pitrè, IV, 236.
Eng. *You cheat an old woman once: the next time she shuts the door on you.*

gaddina *n.f.* hen, chicken.
Gatti e gaddini, lu Signuri si nni ridi. Source: Pitrè, IV, 216.
Eng. *Don't sweat the small stuff.* **Lit.** *At cats and chickens, the Lord chuckles.*

gàggia *n.f.* cage, birdcage, chicken coop, a quantity of birds, creel, mousetrap, fig. prison.
Stu munnu è 'na gàggia di pazzi. Source: Pitrè, IV, 190.
Eng. *This world is a cage of fools.*

galanti *adj.* gallant, heroic, chivalrous.
Nun vogghiu fari tantu lu galanti,

Cà tempu veni misiru e pizzenti. Source: Pitrè, IV, 127.
Eng. *I don't want to play the gallant,*
For the time will come when I am wretched and a beggar.

galantomu *n.m.* gentleman.
A un galantomu ogni paisi è patria. Source: Pitrè, III, 114.
Eng. *A gentleman is at home everywhere.*

giustu *adj.* just, fair.
Lu giustu pecca setti voti lu jornu. Source: Pitrè, IV, 255.
Eng. *The just man sins seven times a day.*

gnuranti *adj.* ignorant.
L'omu sempri apprenni e mori gnuranti. Source: Pitrè, II 179.
Eng. *Man is always learning and dies ignorant.*

governari *v.t.* govern.
Ognunu guverna a sè stissu e Diu guverna a tutti. Source: Traina, 444.
Eng. *Everybody governs himself and God governs over all.*

governu *n.m.* government, guide, direction.
Nun sempri dura lu malu governu. Source: Traina, 444.
Eng. *A bad government doesn't last forever.*

gradigghia *n.f.* grill.
Cci dissi a la padedda la gradigghia:
Iu pisci grossi vogghiu, e no fragagghia. Source: Pitrè, IV, 85.
Eng. *The grill said to the frying pan:*
I want big fishes not minnows.

groi *n.m.* crane.
Quannu passanu li groi, guarda pri li favi. Source: Pitrè, I, 60.
Eng. *When the cranes migrate, it's time to plant the fava.*
Tr. note: Mina-Palumbo indicates that the cranes migrate over Sicily anytime from about the first of October to the end of November. In Sacramento I plant the fava seeds around the beginning of October for harvesting during April and May, leaving the last few plants to go to seed for planting the following year.

guastidduni *n.m.* type of round bread, bigger than normal.
Di cui speri lu guastidduni
Finciticci puviridduni. Source: Pitrè, IV, 157.

51

Eng. *To someone from whom you hope for generous help*
Pretend great poverty.
Lit. *To someone from whom you hope for a big round loaf of bread*
Pretend great poverty.
Tr. note: This proverb is in Chapter LXXXVII on *Various practical rules of conduct for life.*

gustu *n.m.* taste, pleasure.
De gustibus non est disputatu. (*Noto*). Source: Pitrè, I, 16.
Eng. *To each his own.*
Lit. *There's no accounting for taste.*

imbrugghiari *v.r.* become entangled.
Cui camina drittu nun si 'mmrògghia. Source: Pitrè, III, 281.
Eng. *He who walks the straight and narrow avoids entanglements.*

imprescia *adv.* quickly, suddenly.
Megghiu scumunicatu a tortu chi cumunicatu a la 'mprescia. Source: Pitrè, IV, 25.
Eng. *It's better to be wrongfully excommunicated than to receive last rites in a hurry.*

incignusu *adj.* ingenious.
La puvirtà fa l'omu 'ncignusu; Source: Pitrè, III, 262.
Eng. *Necessity is the mother of invention.*
Lit. *Poverty makes a man ingenious.*

inciùria *n.f.* insult, injury, offense.
Summa giustizia, summa 'nciùria. Source: Pitrè, II, 334.
Eng. *Summary justice is a summary offense.*
Tr. note: This proverb is in Pitrè, Volume II, Chapter 45, Justice, Argument.

ingannu *n.m.* deception, fraud, guile.
Raru guadagnu c'è senza lu 'ngannu.
Eng. *There is rarely gain without deception.*

isca *n.f.* enticement, food, bait.
Ammàtula si pisca si all'amu nun c'è isca. Source: Copani, 199.
Eng. *It's pointless to fish if there's no bait on the hook.*
Tr. note: Copani suggests that today's usage is more pessimistic and concerns pay-offs.

Invanu si pisca si all' amu non cc'é l'isca. Source: Traina, 508.
English proverb. You need to bait the hook to catch the fish.
Lit. *You fish in vain if you don't bait the hook.*

iurari *v.i.* take an oath, swear, pledge.
Lu celu e la terra l'ha ghiuratu chi nun cc'è cosa cui nun s'ha saputu.
Source: Traina, 853.
Eng. *The truth will out.*
Lit. *Heaven and earth have pledged that there is nothing that will not be revealed.*

jancu *adj.* white. *Also: iancu, bbiàncu, bbrancu, ulancu, viàncu.*
Li parrini di niuru ti la jèttanu, di jancu ti carrìanu.
Eng. *Priests dressed in black bring bad tidings; in white they take you to the cemetery.*

jardinu *n.m.* garden.
Jardinu senza cani, è senza patruni. Source: Pitrè, I, 46.
Eng. *A garden without a dog is without an owner.*

jencu *n.m.* bullock, young castrated bull, steer.
Lu jencu fuj a la vista di lu tàuru. Source: Bellantonio, II 155.
Eng. The bullock flees at the sight of the bull.

Lu jencu 'mpara di lu voi, e la vitedda di la vacca. Source: Bellantonio, II 155.
Eng. The steer learns from the oxen, and the calf from the cow.

jiditu *n.m.* finger.
Li jidita di la manu nun su' tutti pari. Source: Pitrè, III, 125.
Eng. The fingers of the hand are not all the same.

Jinnaru *n.m.* January.
Cci havi a pinsari jinnaru quannu havi a chioviri.
Eng. Plan ahead.
Lit. January needs to consider when it should rain.

La luna di jinnaru luci comu jornu chiaru.
Eng. The January moon turns night into day.

jittari *v.t.* throw. *Also: ittari.*
Jittari pruvuli 'ntall' occhi. Source: Traina, 784.
Eng. He was just blowing smoke.
Lit. Throwing dust into the eyes.

Ogni cani ch' abbaja jèttacci 'na petra. Source: Pitrè, II, 405.
Eng. Throw a stone at every dog that barks.

jornu *n.m.* day, daybreak, daylight.
Jornu mai fu chi nun scurassi. Source: Pitrè, II, 288.
Eng. There's never been a day without nightfall.

jurnata *n.f.* day.
Lu voi ca si mancia la pagghiata, lavura tutta la jurnata.
Eng. The ox that eats the hay works the entire day.

lassari *v.t.* leave, abandon, part.
Comu si pigghia lu munnu si lassa. Source: Pitrè, III, 246.
Eng. Leave the world the way you find it.

Nun ti fidari chi la corda è grossa,
Quant' è cchiù grossa, cchiù prestu si lassa. Source: Pitrè, IV, 119.
Eng. *Don't count on the thickness of the rope,*
The thicker it is, the sooner it will part.

làstima *n.f.* affliction, annoyance, pain, anguish.
Ognunu havi li so' làstimi. Source: Pitrè, III, 94.
Eng. *Everyone has his own afflictions.*

latru *n.m.* thief.
La cummudità fa l' omu latru. Source: Pitrè, III, 379.
Eng. *Convenience makes the man a thief.*
L'occasioni fa l' omu latru. Source: Pitrè, III, 379.
Eng. *The occasion makes the man a thief.*

laudari *v.t.* praise.
Si lauda lu fini di la vita, e lu jornu quannu scura. Source: Pitrè, IV, 186.
Eng. *A life is praised at its end, and a day is praised after nightfall.*

lavannara *n.f.* washerwoman.
A bona lavannara nun manca petra. Source: Pitrè, III, 188.
Eng. *The good washerwoman doesn't lack for a washboard.*

lavuraturi *n.m.* worker.
Un bonu lavuraturi, sempri è chiamatu a lavurari. Source: Pitrè, III, 188.
Eng. *A good worker is always picked to work.*

lavuri *n.m.* crops, plants, stalks, seedlings.
L'acqua assai fa curcari li lavuri. Source: Pitrè, I, 47.
Eng. *A lot of water makes the crops fall over.*
Pitrè explains that this is yet another example of every excess being a vice.

Si lu lavuri si curca, lu patruni si susi. Source: Traina, 527.
Eng. *When the crop ripens, the owner begins the harvest.*
Lit. *When the wheat goes to bed the owner rises.*

libbirtati *n.f.* liberty, freedom.
Libbirtati e saluti cu' ha, è riccu e nun lu sa. Source: Pitrè, IV, 8.
Eng. He *who has freedom and health is rich and doesn't know it.*

lignu *n.m.* wood, stick, roof beam, lever, ship, fig. stubborn.
Purtari lignu a lu voscu. Source: Traina, 534.
Eng. *Carrying coals to Newcastle.*
Lit. *Carrying wood to the forest.*

liuni *n.m.* lion.
Ogni cani è liuni a la so' casa. Source: Traina, 149.
Eng. *Every dog is a lion in his own house.*
Tr. note: The two versions of this proverb, by Pitrè and by Traina, have very different meanings.

Ogni cani e liuni havi la sò casa. Source: Pitrè, I, 135.
Eng. *Every dog and lion has its own house.*
Tr. note: The two versions of this proverb, by Pitrè and by Traina, have very different meanings.

lordu *adj.* gross, dirty, filthy, foul.
A paroli lordi, oricchi sirrati. Source: Pitrè, III, 315.
Eng. *At foul language, close your ears.*

Nun si tocca l'oru cu li manu lordi. Source: Pitrè, IV, 147.
Eng. *Honor the virtuous.*
Lit. *Don't touch gold with dirty hands.*

lupu *n.m.* wolf.
Sutta peddi d'agneddu lupu rapaci. Source: Pitrè, IV, 71.
Eng. *A wolf in sheep's clothing.*

macàri *conj.* also, even, even if, though.
Avissi, fussi e **macari** su' tri cosi chi nuddu nni voli. Source: Pitrè, I, 12.
Eng. *If I had, if I were, and, even if, are three things nobody wants to hear.*

maccarruni *n.m.* macaroni, hollow pasta, shaped pasta, fig. ignoramus.
Guai e maccarruna si mancianu càudi. Source: Pitrè, IV, 255.
Eng. *Troubles and macaroni are to be eaten hot.*

Vôi campari anni e annuni?
Vivicci forti supra li maccarruni.
Eng. *Do you want to live a long life?*
Drink wine liberally with macaroni.

maceddu *n.m.* slaughterhouse.
Quannu lu voi è a lu maceddu,
Tutti cùrrinu cu lu cuteddu. Source: Pitrè, III, 96.
Eng. *When the ox is at the slaughterhouse,*
Everyone comes running with a knife.

macinari *v.t.* grind, crush, mince.
Bisogna macinari quannu chiovi. Source: Pitrè, III, 372.
Eng. *Make good use of your time.*
Lit. *You need to grind when it rains.*
Note. If the farmer can't work in the field because of the rain, then he should work on an inside task.

magghiolu *n.m.* bot. shoot, tinder, leafy branch.
D'ogni viti si nni pigghia un magghiolu. Source: Pitrè, I, 44.
Eng. *Take a shoot from each grapevine.*

màghiru *adj.* thin, emaciated, wasting away.
Nun servi la carni tutta grassa,
E mancu tanta màghira cu l'ossa. Source: Pitrè, IV, 102.
Eng. *One wants neither meat that's too fatty,*
Nor too lean and bony.

mai *adv.* never, ever.
La virtù nun mori mai. Source: Pitrè, IV, 147.
Eng. *Virtue never goes out of style.*

Megghiu tardu chi mai. Source: Pitrè, III, 185.
Eng. *Better late than never.*

maidda *n.f.* cupboard, hopper, fish hatchery, trough.
Sparagna la farina, mentri la maidda è china. Source: Bellantonio, II, 109.
Eng. *Conserve the flour while the hopper is still full.*

maisa *n.f.* fallow field.
Si riccu si vò fari lu burgisi,
Simina l' òriu supra lu maisi. Source: Pitrè, I, 67.
Eng. *The farmer who wants to get rich*
Sows barley on a field that's been fallow.

maistrali *n.m.* northwesterly wind.
Ventu maistrali jinchi pùzzura e funtani. Source: Pitrè, III, 38.
Eng. *The northwesterly fills wells and fountains.*

majorca *n.f.* Type of fine grain.
Ti vôi 'nsignari a pagari li detti?
Simina majorca e chianta catarratti (**Castelbuono**). Source: Pitrè, I, 70.
Eng. *Would you like to know how to pay off your debts?*
Sow majorca grain and plant catarratti grapes.

majuri *adj.* bigger, senior, wise.
Supra lu majuri si 'nsigna lu minuri Source: Pitrè, IV, 224.
Eng. *We learn by standing on the shoulders of the wise.*

manu *n.m.* hand, help, cooperation.
Avemu a basari ddi manu chi meritanu di essiri tagghiati.
Eng. *We have to kiss the hands that deserve to be cut off.*

Li multi manu sgravanu travagghiu. Source: Pitrè, III, 203.
Eng. *Many hands make light work.*
Pitrè notes that the author of this proverb was for the division of labor.

Lu megghiu è chiddu chi tegnu a li manu.
Eng. *A bird in the hand is worth two in the bush.*
Lit. *The one I'm holding in my hand is the best.*

maravigghia *n.f.* marvel, wonder, miracle.
Di nuddu nni putemu fari maravigghia. Source: Pitrè, I, 338.
Eng. *We can't be surprised by anyone's deeds.*

La maravigghia, di la 'gnuranza è figghia. Source: Pitrè, IV, 41.
Eng. *Wonder is the handmaiden of ignorance.*

La maravigghia la fa l'omu, ca la fimmina fa lu disiu. Source: Pitrè, IV, 41.
Eng. *The man creates the wonder; the woman creates the desire.*

massara *n.f.* wife of the manager, diligent, thrifty, industrious, prompt, wife of the sexton.
La mugghieri massara è n'autra dota.
Eng. *A diligent housewife is a double dowry.*

matinu *n.m.* dawn, morning, daybreak.
Cui nesci matinu, àscia un carrinu. Source: Pitrè, II, 288.
Eng. *The early bird catches the worm.*
Lit. *One who goes out in the morning finds a coin.)*
Tr. note: This proverb is in Pitrè, Volume II, Chapter 42, Day, Night.

matri *n.f.* mother.
L' amuri di la matri è cecu. Source: Pitrè, II 213.

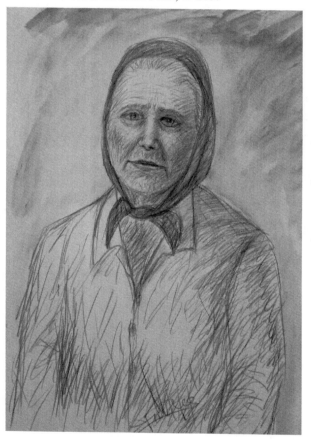

Eng. *A mother's love is blind.*

La matri sempri è matri. Source: Bellantonio, II 152.
Eng. *Mother is always mother.*

Ogni scravagghieddu a so matri pari beddu.
Eng. *Every little beetle looks beautiful to its mother.*

matrimoniu *n.m.* matrimony, marriage.
Lu matrimoniu s'havi a fari o prestu o mai.
Eng. *Marriage must take place early or never.*

Vintott'anni voli aviri l'omu, dicidotto idda: è matrimoniu bonu.
Eng. *It's a good marriage when he's twenty eight and she's eighteen.*

'mpisu *adj.* hanged, unfortunate.
Cui dissi *avissi!* fu 'mpisu. Source: Pitrè, I, 13.
Eng. *The one who said if I had! was hanged.*

Cui mancia cucuzza, mori 'mpisu. Source: Pitrè, III, 218.
Eng. *He who eats squash, dies hanged.*
Pitrè notes: this means that spies who reveal facts about others, risk great danger.

'mprinari *v.t.* impregnate.
Donna maritata, donna 'mprinata. Source: Pitrè, IV, 230.
Eng. *A married woman is a pregnant woman.*

muddichi *n.f.* crumbs.
Cui mancia, fa muddichi. Source: Pitrè, II, 158.
Eng. *Eating makes crumbs.*

Cui mancia fa muddichi, e cui mancia cu cchiù pitittu nni fa cchiù grossi.
Source: Pitrè, II, 158.
Eng. *Whoever eats makes crumbs, and who eats with more of an appetite
will make bigger crumbs.*

Nun si pò manciari senza fari muddichi. Source: Pitrè, II, 158.
Eng. *You can't eat without making crumbs.*
Pitrè adds this extract from Don Chisciotti e Sanciu Panza, Canto IV, stanza 23,
by Giovanni Meli:

"Cui mancia finalmenti fa muddichi,
E qualchi vota lu grand'omu dormi."
Eng. *He who eats will eventually make crumbs,
And sometimes the great man will sleep.*

Tr. note: A translation of this Giovanni Meli book from Sicilian to English by Gaetano Cipolla, is available from Legas in a dual language edition.

mugghieri *n.f.* wife.
Bona terra e bona mugghieri,
Portanu all'omu beni. Source: Pitrè, II, 65.
Eng. Good land and a good wife,
Bring a man well-being.

Detti e mugghieri 'nta stu munnu cu' nun nni voli nun nn'havi.
Eng. Debts and a wife are of your own choosing.
Lit. In this world he who doesn't want debts and a wife, doesn't have them.

mulinu *n.m.* mill.
Cui trasi a lu mulinu, s'infarina. Source: Pitrè, I, 232.
Eng. You're known by the friends you keep.
Lit. One who enters the mill will get covered with flour.
Tr. note: This proverb is in Pitrè, Volume I, Chapter 19, Good And Bad Company.

munciri *v.t.* to milk.
Munci petra ca nesci sucu.
Eng. Squeezing blood out of a stone.

munnu *n.m.* world.
Lassa stari lu munnu comu lu trovi. Source: Pitrè, IV, 165.
Eng. Leave the world the way you find it.

murituri *adj.* mortal, deadly, lethal. Muraturi, murituri. Source: Pitrè, IV, 261.
Eng. Mason, mortal.
Pitrè adds: "Because of the danger they encounter in plying their trade."

nannu *n.m.* grandfather.
Olivari di tò nannu, cèusi di tò patri, vigna tò.
Eng. The olive grove of your grandfather, the mulberry trees of your father, and grape vines that you planted.

Napuli *place name* Naples.
Vidi Palermu e gori, vidi Napuli e poi mori.
Eng. See Palermo and enjoy it; see Naples, then die.

nasciri *v.i.* be born, begin to be.
Si sapi unni si nasci, ma nun si sapi unni si mori.
Eng. *The uncertainty of human existence.*
Lit. *It's known where you were born, but it's not known where you'll die.*

nascunniri *v.t.* hide.
La bona fama nascunni li furti. Source: Pitrè, I, 207.
Eng. *Thefts are hidden by a good reputation.*

nasu *n.m.* nose.
Ogni nasu stà beddu a la sò facci. Source: Pitrè, I, 169.
Eng. *A place for everything and everything in its place.*
Lit. *Each nose fits well on its own face.*
Tr. note: This proverb is in Pitrè, Volume I, Chapter 12, Beauty, Ugliness, Bodily features.

'ncegnu *n.m.* intelligence, brains, wit, talent, facility, creativity.
Nun bastanu l'anni pri sapiri: cci voli lu 'ncegnu. Source: Pitrè, IV, 45.
Eng. *Years don't suffice for learning: you need brains.*
Tr. note: Pitrè adds a quote from Plato,*"Non aetate verum ingenio adipiscitur sapientia."* It is not age but true genius that attains wisdom.

'nchiappa *n.f.* swill, scribble, mess, speck, bungled, mistake.
Li cosi accuminzati cu lu 'nchiappa-'nchià,
Finiscinu cu lu 'nchiappa-'nchiù. Source: Pitrè, IV, 150.
Eng. *You can't make a silk purse out of a sow's ear.*
Lit. *Things started with a mess*
Finish with a greater mess.

nenti *pron.* nothing.
Sutta lu celu nenti cc'è di novu. Source: Pitrè, IV, 190.
Eng. *There is nothing new under the sun.*

Tanti nenti ammazzanu un asinu. Source: Bellantonio, II, 110.
Eng. *Many nothings can kill a jackass.*

nèspula *n.f.* medlar, loquat. Also: **nèspura, nièspula, nièspura, nìspula, nèspulu.**
Quannu viditi nespuli chianciti, ca su l'ultimu fruttu di l'estati.
Eng. *Cry when you see medlars because they're the last fruit of the summer.*

'nfernu *n.m.* hell.
Si vôi pruvari li peni di lu 'nfernu, lu 'nvernu a Missina, e la stati 'n Palermu. Source: Pitrè, III, 168.
Eng. *If you want to experience the pains of hell, spend the winter in Messina and the summer in Palermo.*

ngastu *n.m.* joint, dovetail, slot, recess, eye socket, orbit.
Statti 'ntra lu tò 'ngastu. Source: Pitrè, IV, 174.
Eng. *Stay within your own orbit.*

nolu *n.m.* shipping charge, freight charge.
È cchiù lu nolu chi la mircanzia. Source: Pitrè, I, 318.
Eng. *Shipping costs more than the merchandise.*

'ntressu *n.m.* interest, fin. loan interest.
Unni cc' è 'ntressu, nun cc' è amuri. Source: Pitrè, II, 285.
Eng. *Where money is involved, there's no love.*
Lit. *Where there's loan interest, there's no love.*

'nvicchiri *v.i.* age, grow old.
A tavula nun si 'nvecchia. Source: Pitrè, IV, 83.
Eng. *One doesn't grow old at the table.*

'nvidia *n.f.* envy, jealousy.
La 'nvidia è matri di la 'gnuranza. Source: Pitrè, IV, 244.
Eng. *Jealousy is the mother of ignorance.*

'nzèmmula *adv.* together.
Nuddu arricchisci tuttu 'nsèmmula. Source: Pitrè, III, 272.
Eng. *Nobody gets rich all together.*

'nzirtari *v.t.* foretell, guess, find an exact solution.
L' omu chi si marita, mori e nasci:
E si dici: mischinu cu' la 'nzerta! Source: Pitrè, II, 99.
Eng. *The man who marries dies and is reborn:*
And it is said: Pity the fellow who guessed correctly!

nziru *n.m.* a terra-cotta vase used for liquids, usually without handles.
Quannu figghia nziru e fa nziriddu!
Eng. *When hell freezes over!*

Lit. When the vase gives birth and makes a little vase.

o *conj.* either, or.
O dintra o fora. Source: Pitrè, III, 384.
Eng. Either in or out.

occhiettu *n.m.* buttonhole, eyelet, bump, swelling.
Quantu occhietti, tanti buttuna (Catania). Source: Bellantonio;, II, 108;
Pitrè, II, 147.
Eng. There are as many buttons as there are buttonholes.

olivi *n.f.* olives.
Acqua e nivi fa l'olivi. Source: Pitrè, IV, 245.
Eng. Water and snow make olives grow.

Tri sunnu li nnimici di l'oliva:
Lu sirràculu, vermi e cuttuneddu (**Castelbuono**). Source: Pitrè, i, 71.
Eng. There are three enemies of the olive:
The olive bark beetle, the olive fruit fly, and the olive psyllid.
Pitrè supplies the scientific names: *Phloiotribus oleae, Dacus oleae, and Psylla*
olivetorum.

omini *n.m.* men, people.
L'omini all'àutu e li scecchi a la via. Source: Pitrè, I, 84.
Eng. Men in high places and jackasses along the road recognize each
other.

omu *n.m.* man.
L'omu chi si marita mori e nasci. Source: Pitrè, II, 99.
Eng. The man that marries dies and is reborn.

L'omu è sempri picciottu. Source: Pitrè, II, 305.
Eng. A man is always young.
Tr. note: This proverb is in Pitrè, Volume II, Chapter 43, Youth, Old Age.

L'omu picciottu, 'un si misura a parmu. Source: Pitrè, II, 305.
Eng. You don't measure a young man in hands.

L'omu pri la parola, lu voi pri li corna. Source: Pitrè, III, 282.
Eng. A man for his word, an oxen for his horns.

onuratu *adj.* honest, honorable.
Megghiu poviru onuratu, chi riccu curnutu. Source: Pitrè, IV, 220.
Eng. Better a poor man who is honored than a rich man whose wife cheats on him.

opira *n.f.* work.
Di l'opira si conusci lu mastru. Source: Pitrè, III, 302; IV, 39.
Eng. You know the master by his work.

oriu *n.m.* barley, fig. beating.
Si l'òriu va caru, chi curpa cci havi la mula? Source: Bellantonio, II, 109.
Eng. What fault is it of the mule if the cost of barley goes up?

ovu *n.m.* egg.
Megghiu oj l'ovu chi dumani la gaddina. Source: Pitrè, III, 381.
Eng. Better an egg today than the hen tomorrow.

pacenzia *n.f.* forbearance, patience.
Oricchi di mircanti e pacenzia di santi. Source: Pitrè, IV, 160.
Eng. You need to have the ears of merchants and the patience of saints.

Pacenzia cci voli a li burraschi: nun si mancia meli senza muschi. Source: Zinna, 122.
Eng. You need to have patience during storms: you don't eat honey without flies.

paci *n.f.s.* peace, tranquility, serenity, quiet, patience, slowness.
Ddoppu la guerra è cchiù cara la paci. Source: Pitrè, IV, 215.
Eng. After the war, peace is more appreciated.
Pitrè explains: "Dicesi delle guerre d'amore."
Eng. Said of the wars of love. Lover's spats.

pagatu *v.t. past p.* paid.
Cu' ha travagghiatu, vol'essiri pagatu.
Eng. The worker wants to be paid.

Robba circata, robba pagata. Source: Pitrè, IV, 384.
Eng. Goods sought, goods bought.

pagghia *n.f.* straw, hay.

Cavaddu di focu, omu di pagghia,
Cavaddu di pagghia; omu di focu. Source: Pitrè, I, 124.
Eng. *A spirited horse, wastes the rider,*
An intemperate rider, wastes the horse.
Pitrè notes: "Il caval focoso consuma il cavalcatore; il cavalcatore intemperante
rovina il cavallo.
Eng. A spirited horse wastes the rider; an intemperate rider ruins the horse.

paladinu *n.m.* paladin.
Eng. *One of Charlemagne's twelve knights.*
Tr. note: The maker of the puppets, ***pupi*** in Sicilian, is called ***u puparu***, pictured
here with one of his creations. The puppet shows, ***opira dî pupi***, recount the battles
of the paladins Rinaldo and Orlando, against the Saracens.

palatu *n.m.* palate.
Nun tutti hannu lu stissu palatu. Source: Pitrè, I, 22.
Eng. *There's no accounting for taste.*

palora *n.f.* word, pledge.
La prima palora è ancilu.
Eng. *Words are for reasoning.*
Lit. *The first word is an angel.*

Palori e pinni lu ventu li leva.
Eng. *Actions speak louder than words.*
Lit. *Words and feathers are blown away by the wind.*

pampinedda *n.f. dim.* leaf.
Dunni va la pampinedda,
Nun cci va la muddichedda (**Menfi**). Source: Pitrè, IV, 259.
Eng. *Where one thing belongs, the other does not.*
Lit. *Where the leaf goes, the crumb does not.*
Pitrè explains this proverb and adds further that the one thing has nothing in common with the other.

panàru *n.m.* basket.
La zappudda di jinnaru si jinchi lu panaru. Source: Pitrè, I, 50.
Eng. *With January hoeing, the basket is filled.*

Nun pigghiari l'acqua 'ntra lu panàru. Source: Pitrè, IV, 171.
Eng. *Don't fetch water with a basket.*

pani *n.m.* bread.
Lu pani nun si lassa. Source: Pitrè, III, 206.
Eng. *Don't leave gainful employment.*
Lit. *Bread is not to be left.*

Lu pani nun veni di lu Gloria Patri. Source: Pitrè, III, 206.
Eng. *You must work to earn your livelihood.*
Lit. *Bread doesn't come from Heaven.*

papà *n.m.* dad, daddy.
U' papà càtta, 'a mammà mùccia, e u' figghiu mucca. Source: Annaro, 311.
Eng. *Daddy buys it, mommy hides it, and the child eats it.*

Tr. note: This is about the sweets that are hidden around the house on All Soul's Day. Much like our Easter Egg hunts. The Sicilian is in the parlata of Caltagirone, where Annaro was the pastor of the parish of St. George, the long time home parish of our branch of the Dieli family.

para *n.f.* shield, parry.
Lu para e fuj è sarvamentu di vita. Source: Pitrè, III, 242.
Eng *To parry and flee is lifesaving.*

paraguni *n.m.* comparison.
Li paraguni su' udiusi. Source: Pitrè, III, 323.
Eng. Comparisons are hateful.

parrastra *n.f.* stepmother.
La stati è la parrastra di li picciriddi. Source: Pitrè, III, 33.
Eng. Summer is the stepmother of little children.
Tr. note: Pitrè says it's because children get all kinds of illnesses during the summer.

parrastru *n.m.* stepfather.
Lu 'Nvernu è lu parrastru di li puvireddi. Source: Pitrè, III, 37.
Eng. Winter is the stepfather of the poor.
Pitrè notes: In winter the poor experience cold, hunger, and many other troubles.

parturiri *v.t.* give birth. *Also: figghiari.*
La virità parturisci odiu. Source: Pitrè, IV, 57.
Eng. Truth gives birth to hate.

pastizzaru *n.m.* pastry chef, confectioner, candymaker.
Cc' è bisognu chi si licca la mugghieri di lu pastizzaru! Source: Pitrè, I, 19.
Eng. The pastry chef's wife needs to taste the sweets!

pàtiri *v.i.* suffer, endure, experience pain, tolerate.
Comu nun vôi pàtiri, nun fari. Source: Pitrè, IV, 147.
Eng. Do unto others as you would have others do unto you.
Lit. As you would not want to suffer, don't do.

patri *n.m.* father.
Lu diavulu è patri di la minzogna. Source: Pitrè, IV, 59.
Eng. The devil is the father of the lie.

Patri Lanuzza *n.m.* Father Lanuzza
Nè 'ntra la casa, nè 'mmenzu la chiazza,
Nun stati a fari lu Patri Lanuzza. Source: Pitrè, IV, 167.
Eng. *Either in the house or in the public square,*
Don't act like Father Lanuzza.
Tr. note: Father Lanuzza (1591-1655) was a Jesuit from the town of Licata who led an exemplary life and never tired of preaching. He travelled all over Sicily, preaching against vices. He was so popular that the people could not be accomodated in the biggest churches so he preached in the public squares. In Palermo itself, his audience, on several occasions exceeded 25,000.

patruni *n.m.* boss, master, owner.
Rispetta a lu patruni rispetta a lu cani.
Eng. *Love me, love my dog.*
Lit. *Respect the owner, respect the dog.*

paura *n.f.* fear.
Cu' havi paura, si salva. Source: Pitrè, IV, 377.
Eng. *He who has fear will be saved.*

pazzu *n.m.* crazy, insane.
Cui spera limòsina di parrini, va a lu spitali pri pazzi. Source: Alaimo, 153.
Eng. *He who hopes for alms from the priests winds up at the insane asylum.*

pècuri *n.pl.* sheep, sheepfold.
Quannu vai a pècuri e t'arrinesci,
Pigghia la grossa cà la nica crisci. Source: Pitrè, II, 285.
Eng. *When you're taking from the sheepfold and you're succeeding,*
Take the big one because the small one will grow.
Tr. note: Pitrè adds that this is advice for the thief, so that by the time he makes a second foray, the smaller sheep will have grown.

pedi *n.m.* foot, feet.
Cui va a pedi 'ntra aprili e maju, va a cavaddu tuttu l'annu.
Eng. *Whoever goes on foot during April and May, goes on horseback the rest of the year.*

peju *adj. adv.* worse, worst. Also: **peiu**, **peggiu**.
Cui cància la vecchia pri la nova, peju trova. Source: Pitrè, II, 175.
Eng. *He who leaves the old for the new finds worse.*

Tr. note: In modern technology, this is often referred to as the bleeding edge by adopters of a new version of an old standby.

persu *adj.* lost.
Lu persu è persu. Source: Pitrè, IV, 183.
Eng. What's lost, is lost.

piaciri *v.i.* pleasure, delight, like, please, favor, service.
Li cosi duci piacinu a tutti. Source: Pitrè, IV, 65.
Eng. Everyone likes sweet things.

pica *n.f.* spear, pike, lance.
Nun tutti su' boni surdati chiddi chi 'n coddu portanu la pica. Source: Bellantonio, II 137.
Eng. Not all those who shoulder a spear are good soldiers.

picca *adj.* few, little.
Megghiu picca chi nenti. Source: Pitrè, IV, 124.
Eng. Half a loaf is better than none.
Lit. Less is better than nothing.

picciriddi *n.pl.* little children.
Voi sapiri la virità? Dumanna a li picciriddi. Source: Bellantonio, II 169.

Eng. *If you want to know the truth, ask the children.*

picuntria *n.f.* hypochondria
La picontria è cchiù tinta di 'na malatia. Source: Zinna, 106.
Eng. *Hypochondria is worse than a sickness.*

Piddirinu *n.m.* Pellegrino.
Quannu veni di Munti Piddirinu,
Pigghia la robba e ti la càrrichi supra lu schinu. Source: Pitrè, III, 57.
Eng. *When clouds come from Mount Pellegrino,*
Pick up your things and leave because rain is on the way.
Lit. *Pick up your things and carry them on your back.*

pidudda *n.f.* gut.
Pani e cipudda jinchi la pidudda. Source: Pitrè, IV, 105.
Eng. *Bread and onion fill the gut.*

piduni *n.m.* pedestrian.
Cu' è a cavaddu, salutassi li piduna. Source: Pitrè, III, 329.
Eng. *The one on horseback should greet pedestrians.*

pigghiari *v.t.* get, take, seize, have.
Mentri hai bon tempu pigghiatillu,
Chi lu malu tempu nun manca mai. Source: Pitrè, III, 386.
Eng. *Take the good time while it lasts,*
For a bad time is never lacking.

Pileri *n.m.* pile of stones, plover, Selinunte.
Nun chiamari ventu a mari,
E mancu suli a lu Pileri (Castelvetrano). Source: Pitrè, III, 56.
Eng. *Don't call for wind at sea,*
*Nor for sun at Selinunte (**Castelvetrano**).*
Pitrè explains: Pileri is how the local population refers to the temple ruins of
Selinunte.

pinciri *v.t.* paint, fantasize, praise, refl. put make-up on.
Un bonu maritu ti pinci, un tintu maritu ti tinci. Source: Pitrè, IV, 233.
Eng. *A good husband praises you; a bad husband maligns you.*
Lit. *A good husband paints you; a bad husband stains you.*

pinìa *v.i.* suffers.
Si marzu nun marzìa, giugnu pinìa.
Eng. *If March is late in coming, June will suffer.*

pinitenza *n.f.* penal satisfaction, penance.
La vicchiaja è pinitenza. Source: Pitrè, IV, 379.
Eng. *Old age is penance.*

pinna *n.f.* feather, quill pen, small sail, .
La pinna pisa cchiù di la zappa. Source: Pitrè, IV, 379.
Eng. A quill pen weighs more than a hoe.
Pitrè adds: "La dottrina vuole assai più fatica che la terra."
Eng. Scholarship requires a lot more work than farming.

pinzari *v.t.* think, contrive, devise, believe, esteem, remember. Also: **pinsari**.
Cui voli ben parrari, bisogna ben pinsari. Source: Pitrè, III, 221.
Eng. *Think before you speak.*
Lit. *One who wishes to speak well needs to think well.*

pipi *n.m. inv.* pepper, chili pepper, spice pepper.
Cu' ha pipi, metti a li càuli. Source: Pitrè, IV, 86.
Eng. *He who has pepper puts it on the cabbages.*
Pitrè notes: "Of one who incites enmity, hatred, etc., in persons already strongly detested, it is said: *puts pepper on the cabbages.*"

pira *n.f.* pear.
Annata di pira, annata di suspira.
Eng. *A bountiful pear harvest, a year of worry.*
Pitrè notes that farmers have observed that a bountiful pear harvest is accompanied by shortages of more important produce.

pirdizioni *n.f.* danger, ruin, damnation, perdition.
Cui pirduna a sò figghiu l'erruri, lu metti a la pirdizioni. Source: Pitrè, II, 145.
Eng. *One who excuses the errors of his son puts him at risk of damnation.*

pirfettu *adj.* perfect.
Lu fattu è nnimicu di lu pirfettu. Source: Pitrè, IV, 122.
Eng. *Done is the enemy of perfect.*

Pirinnellu *name* Pirandello. Camilleri, 79.
Mi parinu cosi di Pirinnellu.
Eng. These seem to be things of a Pirandellian sort.

pirirà *v.i.* disappear, discourage, die, perish.
Pri la suverchia cummudità la riligioni pirirà.
Eng. Religion will perish because of excessive comforts.

pirtusu *n.m.* hole.
Lu chiovu grossu fa lu pirtusu. Source: Pitrè, IV, 182.
Eng. A big nail makes a hole.

pisari *v.i.t.* weigh, consider.
Pisa giustu e vinni caru. Source: Pitrè, I, 313; Traina, 741.
Eng. Weigh fairly and sell dearly.
Traina notes that it's eqitable; because if the weight is accurate the price is fair.

piscari *v.t.* fish, seek, try to learn, squeal; *(v.i.)* flirt.
A ciumi mortu nun jiri a piscari. Source: Pitrè, IV, 66.
Eng. Don't fish in a dead river.
Tr. note: This proverb is included by Pitrè in his chapter on lying and hypocrisy in volume 4. The dead river refers to a man who is silent and brooding. In Julius Caesar, I, 2, Shakespeare said it this way: "Yon Cassius has a lean and hungry look. He thinks too much. Such men are dangerous."

pitanza *n.f.* portion, course, dish, share, offering.
Si vuliti l'osservanza, dàtinni la pitanza.
Eng. If you want a mass to be celebrated, make an offering.

pitrusinu *n.m.* parsley.
A San Franciscu (4 ottobri) si simìna lu pitrusinu. Source: Pitrè, I, 30.
Eng. On St. Francis Day, October 4, you sow parsley.

pittura *n.f.* the art, technique, activity of painting; a painting, fig. faithful description.
Secunnu è la paga, tali è la pittura. Source: Pitrè, II, 536.
Eng. The means determines the product.
Lit. The work is determined by the price.
Tr. note: This proverb is in Pitrè, Volume II, Chapter 48, Earnings, Wages.

pizzicata *n.f.* pinch, small quantity, pluck of a string

Parturenti e malati
Si cci sta 'na pizzicata. Source: Pitrè, III, 328.
Eng. *With an expectant mother or a sick person*
Keep your visit short.

pizzuddu *n.m.* piece, bit.
Li malatii a vèniri stannu un pizzuddu, ma a jirisinni stannu un seculu.
Source: Pitrè, IV, 17.
Eng. *Sicknesses take just a bit to arrive, but take a century to leave.*

Platuni *name* Plato 427?-347 B.C.
Dici Platuni:
La passioni vinci la raggiuni. Source: Pitrè, I, 16.
Eng. *Plato says:*
Passion overcomes reason.

ponnu *v.i.* able to, can.
Li ricchi comu vonnu e li poviri comu ponnu.
Eng. *The rich do as they want; the poor do as they can.*

portu *n.m.* harbor, port.
A tempu di timpestu, ogni tintu pirtusu è portu. Source: Pitrè, I, 198.

Eng. *Any port in a storm.*
Lit. *During a storm, any stinking hole is a port.*

Cui voli manciari pisci di portu, nun voli aviri lu vurzuni strittu.
Eng. *If you want to eat freshly caught fish, you don't want to have a tight purse.*

potiri *v.i.* be able to.
L'amicu nun è sempri amicu; si pò fari nnimicu. Source: Pitrè, II< 185.
Eng. *A friend isn't always a friend; a friend can become an enemy.*

poviru *adj.* poor.
A lu poviru Diu l'ajuta. Source: Pitrè, I, 275.
Eng. *God will help the poor.*

prèscia *n.f.* hurry, haste.
A cu' ha prèscia, ogn' ura cci pari cent'anni. Source: Pitrè, III, 313.
Eng. *To one in a hurry, each hour seems like a hundred years.*

pridicaturi *n.m.* preacher.
Lu bon pridicaturi divi prima pridicari a sè stissu. Source: Traina, 760.
Eng. *The good preacher practices what he preaches.*
Lit. *The good preacher must first preach to himself.*

priggiudiziu *n.m.* prejudice, bias
Cui si cautela nun fa priggiudiziu. Source: Pitrè, III, 288.
Eng. *Acting with caution is not prejudicial.*
Lit. *Acting with caution is not being biased.*

primintìu *adj.* premature, early, new.
Figghi tardii, orfani primintìi. Source: Pitrè, II, 148.
Eng. *Late children, early orphans.*

principiu *n.m.* beginning, origin, starting.
Lu mali quannu è 'n principiu si sana. Source: Pitrè, III, 380.
Eng. *Time heals all wounds.*
Lit. *The hurt, when it's at the beginning, can be cured.*

Ogni principiu havi lu sò fini. Source: Pitrè, IV, 189.
Eng. *Every begining has its end.*

prisa *n.f.* acquisition, purchase, gain.
Èssiri cchiù la spisa chi la prisa.
Eng. *The expense is more than the gain.*

privari *v.t.* deprive.
Cosa privata genira appititu. Source: Pitrè, I, 13.
Eng. *Deprivation breeds appetite.*

propriu *adj.* own, typical, fitting, appropriate.
Cui vivi mali, lu sò propriu mali l'accusa. Source: Pitrè, IV, 151.
Eng. *One who lives recklessly will suffer by his own doing.*

prudenza *n.f.* prudence, caution.
Cu' havi prudenza, la mostra. Source: Pitrè, IV, 377.
Eng. *One who is prudent. demonstrates prudence.*

prumèttiri *v.t.* to promise.
Nun prumettiri cosi, chi nun pòi attenniri. Source: Pitrè, III, 284.
Eng. *Don't promise what you can't deliver.*

pruverbiu *n.m.* proverb, brief saying, brilliant.
Li pruverbi su' tutti pruvati. Source: Pitrè, I, 1.
Eng. *The proverbs are all proven.*

Lu pruverbiu anticu, è lu Vancèliu nicu. Source: Pitrè, I, 1.
Eng. *Ancient proverbs are a little Gospel.*

pruvidiri *v.t.* supply, provide, furnish.
Cui previdi, pruvidi. Source: Pitrè, III, 291.
Eng. *One who foresees, provides.*

pruvuli *n.f.* gunpowder.
Lu pruvuli ristritta fa un fracassu. Source: Pitrè, II, 12.
Eng. *Restricted gunpowder makes a boom.*

prùvvuli *n.f.* dust.
Cui offenni, scrivi 'n prùvvuli, cu' è offisu, scrivi 'n marmuru.
Eng. *The offender writes in dust; the offended carves it in stone.*
Lit. *The offended writes in marble.*

pudagra *n.f.* gout.
La pudagra è mali di li ricchi. Source: Pitrè, IV, 15.
Eng. Gout is the sickness of the rich.

puddicina *n.f.* chick.
Cui cunta puddicini, cunta pìrita (Palermo). Source: Pitrè, I, 127.
Eng. Don't count your chickens before they mature.
Lit. He who counts chicks, counts farts.
Tr. note: In Palermo they didn't count their chicks even after they hatched because many chicks never matured into chickens.

Cu' havi figghi, havi puddicini. Source: Pitrè, II, 142.
Eng. He wwo has infants, has chicks.
Pitrè points out, because in those days infants could die from one moment to the next.
Tr. note: During the late 1800s, about the time that Pitrè is writing, six of my paternal grandmother's children died before the age of 2.

pugna *n.m.* fist, fistful, punch.
Nun si pò pigghiari lu celu a pugna.
Eng. You can't punch your way into heaven.

pulizìa *v.t.* cleans.
La malatia, si nun guasta, pulizìa. Source: Pitrè, IV, 256.
Eng. If the sickness doesn't kill, it cleanses.
Pitrè takes the meaning of *pulizia* more seriously, probably because of his experience as a practicing physician, when he adds: "If the sickness doesn't end in the death of some person it results in their ruin, because it empties the familiy's pockets as well as their savings."

puntaloru *n.m.* prod, goad, awl, bodkin, tap, dibble.
Cu lu mè puntaloru càcciu lu sceccu,
E cu lu mè quattru tarì fazzu lu saccu. Source: Pitrè, III, 260.
Eng. With my goad I drive the donkey,.
And with my two bucks I fill the sack.

puntu *n.m.* stitch, point, principle, dot, period, moment, spot.
L'omu havi ad aviri un puntu. Source: Pitrè, IV, 182.
Eng. Man needs a focus.
Pitrè explains: "That is to say, a principle to inform or direct his actions."

Puòddina *n.f.* Pollina.
Puòddina caput mundi,
Roma secundi (**Castelbuono**). Source: Pitrè, IV, 383.
Eng. Pollina, the first in the world,
Rome, second.

Siti puddinoti o cristiani? Source: Pitrè, IV, 383.
Eng. Are you from Pollina or are you Christian?

puppa *n.f.* stern, aft.
Anchi cu lu ventu 'n puppa bisogna sapiri navigari. Source: Pitrè, III, 287.
Eng. Even with a tailwind you need to know how to navigate.

purcedda *n.f.* sow, piglet.
Quannu ti dùnanu la purcedda, curri prestu cu la curdicedda. Source: Pitrè,
III, 388.
Eng. Make the most of every opportunity.
Lit. When they give you a piglet, run there quickly with a little leash.

purceddu *n.m.* pig, porker.
Mussu di purceddu, oricchi di mircanti e spaddi di asineddu. Source: Pitrè,
IV, 160.
Eng. You need to have the snout of a pig, the ears of a merchant and the
shoulders of a donkey.

purciara *n.f.* insect ridden, porcelain, purslane.
Annata purciara, annata furmintara.
Eng. When there are lots of insects, look for a good grain year.
Pitre notes that the term is derived from "pulici" which means flea. Picitto defines
"purciara" as meaning either porcelain or the annual grass, purslane and makes no
mention, under this heading, of the flea derivation.

purificari *v.t.* to purify, cleanse, purge.
Lu focu purifica. Source: Pitrè, II, 13.
Eng. Fire purefies.

purpa *n.f.* meat, flesh, substance.
La purpa va cull'ossa. Source: Traina, 782.
Eng. Good things come accompanied with bad things.
Lit. The meat comes with a bone.

purtari *v.t.* carry, bring, take.
Aperta è la porta pri chiddu chi porta. Source: Pitrè, II, 24.
Eng. *Open is the door to the one who is bringing a gift.*

'Na parola porta l'àutra Source: Pitrè, III, 228.
Eng. *One word leads to another.*

Trasìti si purtati. Source: Pitrè, II, 24.
Eng. *Enter if you're bearing a gift.*

puseri *n.m.* thumb.
Vali cchiù lu jiditeddu di lu riccu, chi lu puseri di lu poviru. Source: Pitrè, III, 278.
Eng. *The rich man's pinky is worth more than the poor man's thumb.*

putari *v.t.* to prune.
Cui puta 'ntra Marzu, o è asinu o è pazzu. Source: Pitrè, I, 39.
Eng. *He who prunes in March is either a jackass or is crazy.*

putenza *n.f.* power.
Ogni diavulu voli mustrari la sò putenza. Source: Pitrè, I, 85.
Eng. *Every devil wants to show his power.*

putìa *n.f.* shop, store, business.
Amicu di bon tempu e di putia
Nun è 'na bona e duci cumpagnia. Source: Pitrè, I, 88.
Eng. *A good time or business friend*
Is not a good and endearing companion.

putiri *v.i.* can, able, may, be permitted.
Tutti cosi a stu munnu 'un si ponnu sapiri. Source: Pitrè, IV, 47.
Eng. *In this world you can't know everything.*

putruni *adj.. n.m/f.* loafer, slow, sluggish, lazy.
Cummudità fa l'omu putruni. Source: Pitrè, III, 200.
Eng. *The man who has it easy becomes lazy.*

puvireddu *n.m.* a poor person.
Cu' è picciutteddu, nun è puvireddu.
Eng. *A youngster is never poor.*

puvirtà *n.f.* poverty. Also: **puvirtati** .
A lu poviru puvirtà, a lu riccu ricchizza. Source: Pitrè, III, 252.
Eng. *To the poor man, poverty; to the rich man, riches.*

puzzu *n.m.* well.
Lu pazzu jetta la petra 'ntra lu puzzu, e deci savii la vonnu nèsciri fora.
Source: Pitrè, IV, 50.
Eng. *The madman throws a stone in the well, and ten wise men want to retrieve it.*
Tr. note: "Said especially in reference to scandals and discords." Capponi.
Quannu pri tanta scarsizza di lazzu, quannu pri tanta funnizza di puzzu.
Eng. *Sometimes the rope is too short; sometimes the well is too deep.*

puzzu sfunnatu *adj.* bottomless well, insatiable person.
La casa di lu poviru è puzza sfunnatu. Source: Pitrè, III, 262.
Eng. *The house of the poor man has an insatiable need.*
Lit. *The house of the poor man is a well without a bottom.*

quadara *n.m.* a big vase or pot used for boiling, made of copper or other metal.
Chi fa 'na stizza d'acqua 'ntra 'na quadara vugghienti? Source: Pitrè, II, 12.
Eng. *What will one drop do in a pot of boiling water?*

La quadara vecchia è china di vozzi, pirtusa, e taccuna. Source: Pitrè, II, 301.
Eng. *The old always have ailments.*
Lit. *The old pot is full of nicks, holes, and dents.*

quadaruni *n.m.* large copper pot.
Cui manna carni a la casa cu frati,
Sempri nni trova un quadaruni cchiui. Source: Pitrè, IV, 259.
Eng. *Whoever sends meat to the monastery,*
Will always find another big copper pot there.
Tr. note: Also spelled *quaddaruni*.

quagghia *n.f.* quail.
Fari vulari la quagghia. Source: Attanasio, 44.
Eng. *Let the deal go forward.*
Lit. *Let the quail fly.*

quannu *adv.* when, sometimes.
Cui nun voli quannu pò, nun purrà quannu voli.
Eng. One who doesn't want to when he can, can't when he wants to.

quantu *n.m., adj., adv.* as much as, as far as, how much, as long as.
Casa pi quantu stai, vigna pi quantu vivi, terra pi quantu vidi, e rènnita pi quantu pòi.
Eng. A house for as long as you're here, a vineyard for as long as you live, land for as far as you can see, and income for as much as you can.

quarchi *indef. adj.* some, a few, any.
'Un è tantu dottu lu dottu ch' 'un fazza quarchi erruri. Source: Pitrè, IV, 47.
Eng. He's not so very learned that he doesn't make some errors.

quaresima *n.f.* lent.
Marzu nun veni mai senza quaresima. Source: Pitrè, III, 42.
Eng. March never comes without Lent.

quattru *adj.* four.
Quattr'omini cci vonnu pri fari 'na bona 'nzalata: un pazzu, un saviu, un avaru, e un sfragaru. Source: Pitrè, IV, 108.
Eng. You need four men to make a good salad: a crazy man to mix it, a scholar for the salt, a miser for a touch of vinegar, and a squanderer for the oil.

Quattru e quattru fannu ottu. Source: Pitrè, IV, 63.
Eng. The truth speaks for itself.
Lit. Four and four make eight.
Tr. note: Pitrè put this proverb in his chapter on truth and lies.

Quattru tarì *n.m.* silver coin.
Amicu veru e lu veru parenti,
È lu quattru tarì cu l'ali bianchi Source: Pitrè, III, 266.
Eng. The silver coin with the white wings
Is a true friend and a true relative.
Note by Pitrè: Carlo V introduced the Quatru tarì in 1552. It pictured an eagle with outstretched wings, the symbol used on Sicilian money during the Aragon dynasties.

R *17th letter* R.
Nun jiri a lu suli 'nta li misi chi cc' è la **R**. Source: Pitrè, IV, 246.
*Eng. Stay out of the sun during the months with an **R**.*

racina *n.f.* grapes.
Cogghi appena matura la racina cu bonu tempu e asciutta d'acquazzina.
Source: Traina, 795.
Eng. *Harvest the grapes as soon as they mature; with good weather and after the morning dew.*

radici *n.f.* roots, origin, heritage, source.
Àrvulu ch' 'un fa fruttu, tàgghialu di li ràdichi. Source: Pitrè, I, 30.
Eng. *If the tree doesn't bear fruit, cut it off at the roots.*

Pani e radici;
Zoccu si senti nun si dici. Source: Pitrè, III, 229.
Eng. *At the table and among the family;*
What's heard should not be repeated.

ragghiu *n.m.* bray, braying.
Lu ragghiu di l'asinu nun acchiana 'n celu. Source: Pitrè, IV, 46.
Eng. *The braying of the donkey doesn't reach heaven.*

raggiuni *n.f.* reason.
Cui nun senti raggiuni, nun pò fari cosi cu raggiuni.
Eng. One *who doesn't listen to reason can't do things with reason.*

rallintari *v.t.* ease, slacken, relax, relent.
Erva di ventu ogni mali rallentu.
Eng. *Wild herbs ease every ailment.*

rassimigghjari *v.i.* resemble, be like. *Also rassumigghjari.*
A paisi unni nun si conusciutu,
Comu sì vistu sì rassimigghiatu. Source: Pitrè, IV, 129.
Eng. *In towns where you're not known,*
You're accepted for what you appear to be.

razza *n.f.* race, descent, breed.
Megghiu lu tintu di bona razza,
Ca lu megghiu di tinta razza. Source: Pitrè, I, 133.
Eng. *Better the bad one from a good breed*
Than the best one from a bad breed.

Re Carru *n.m.* silver coins, money.

Quannu cc'è Re Carru 'ntra li manu,
Si fa Pasqua, Natali, e Sammartinu. Source: Pitrè, III, 256.
Eng. *When you have King Charles (money) in your hands,*
You celebrate Easter, Christmas, and the feast of St. Martin.

reda *n.f.* Heredity, lineage, ancestry.
Nè reda senza corna, nè re senza curuna. Source: Pitrè, IV, 186.
Eng. *Neither heirs without horns nor a king without a crown.*

regnari *v.i.* rule, reign, prevail.
È naturali all' omu lu sapiri e lu regnari.
Eng. *It is the nature of man to know and to govern.*

renniri *v.i.* return, render, yield, repay.
Comu paga la zappa,
Accussì l'oliva la spisa renni,
Di la puta, lu grassu, e di la zappa. Source: Pitrè, I, 35.
Eng. *As you pay the price with the hoe,*
To that extent the olive grove will repay you
For the pruning, fertilizing, and hoeing.

riccu *adj.* rich.
Giuvini è cu'è sanu, e riccu cui nun havi a dari.
Eng. *You're young if you're healthy, and rich if you have no debts.*

Quannu lu riccu accarizza lu poviru, signu ca l'havi a 'ngannari.
Eng. *When a rich man caresses a poor man, it's a sign he is going to cheat him.*

Riccu si pò diri cui campa cu lu sò aviri. Source: Pitrè, III, 276.
Eng. *He may be said to be rich who lives within his means.*

ricivu *n.m.* receipt, inheritance.
L'arvulu pecca e la rama ricivi. Source: Pitrè, II, 152.
Eng. *The tree sins and the branch inherits.*

ricotta *n.f.* Sicilian cottage cheese, ricotta.
La ricotta è veru ch' è senz' ossu. Source: Pitrè, IV, 57.
Eng. *It's true that ricotta is boneless.*
Pitrè explains that this proverb is used to counter someone who is saying something

we know is not true.

Latti di crapa, ricotta di pecura e tumazzu di vacca.
Eng. *Milk from the goat, ricotta from the sheep and cheese from the cow.*

ricriari *v.t.* take pleasure, be happy, enjoy.
Ricriati, viddanu,
Mentri la robba è 'n chianu. Source: Pitrè, IV, 213.
Eng. *Farmer, be happy*
When the land you till in the plain.

ridiri *v.i.* laugh, smile.
Cu rid'ò sabbutu chianci 'a duminica.
Eng. *Saturday's revelry leads to Sunday's doldrums.*

Cui sempri ridi è asinu. Source: Pitrè, III, 296.
Eng. *One who always laughs is a jackass.*

riggirusu *adj.* devious, crafty, sneaky, snarly, dupable.
Omu riggirusu a tutti è udiusu. Source: Pitrè, I, 149.
Eng. *The devious man is detested by everyone.*

rimeddiu *n.m.* remedy Also **rimèdiu.**
Fatta la cosa, nun cc'è cchiù rimediu. Source: Pitrè, I, 278.
Eng. *Once it's done, there's no remedy.*

rimitu *n.m.* hermit.
Quannu lu diavulu fu vecchiu si fici rimitu. Source: Pitrè, IV, 70.
Eng. *The old forego the escapades of their youth.*
Lit. *When the devil got old, he became a hermit.*

ringrazziari *v.t.* give thanks, show gratitude.
Ringraziamu a Diu di chiddu chi nni duna, e a lu Re di chiddu chi nni lassa. Source: Pitrè, II, 342.
Eng. *We thank God for what he gives us, and the King for what he leaves us.*
Tr. note: This proverb is in Pitrè, Volume II, Chapter 46, Government, Laws, National Interest.

risplenniri *v.i.* shine, sparkle, glitter, resplendent.
La virtù quantu cchiù è in àutu, tantu cchiù risplenni. Source: Pitrè, IV,

147.
Eng. *The more fervent a virtue, the brighter it shines.*

rispùnniri *v.t.* answer, reply.
Pri 'ngnuranti è tinutu cu' rispuni senza essiri dumannatu.
Eng. *He is regarded ignorant who answers without being asked.*

risu *n.m.* laughter.
Nun ti fidari di cui ti fa la vucca a risu,
Cà mentri ti fa facci ti voli 'mpisu. Source: Pitrè, IV, 70.
Eng. *Don't trust one who smiles at you*
Because while he's smiling, he wants to see you hanged.

ritirata *n.f.* retreat.
Quannu la furtuna vôta,
Ogni amicu si fa la ritirata. Source: Pitrè, III, 96.
Eng. *When fortune turns,*
Every friend retreats.

riturnari *v.i.* return, ruminate, find, recover.
Cu' è di terra, ritorna a la terra. Source: Pitrè, IV, 379.
Eng. *Dust thou art and unto dust thou shalt return.*

riveriri *v.t.* revere, respect, honor, venerate.
Vi rivirìsciu, signuri ciumi,
Ca sàcciu beni li vostri custumi;
Chinu vi trovu e chinu vi lassu,
Si nun chiariti iu nun vi passu. Source: Pitrè, III, 295.
Eng. *Dear river, I respect you,*
For I know all your customs;
Full I find you and full I leave you,
If I can't see your bottom, I won't ford you.

rizzettu *n.m.* refuge, hospitalization, shelter, accommodation, hospitality, domicile.
'U lettu è rizzettu e catalettu. Source: Copani, 130.
Eng. *Bed is both a refuge and a death bed.*
Tr. note: A bed provides a night's rest, but some people die in their sleep.

robba *n.f.* things, property, goods. Also: **roba**.

A la mè robba 'un cci vogghiu patruni. Source: Pitrè, II, 23.
Eng. *I don't want a different owner for my belongings.*
Tr. note: An expression of self interest from the chapter on greed and egotism.

roggi *n.m.* watch, clock, timepiece.
Quannu tri roggi si trovanu equali
Tannu si 'mpenni Puddicinedda. Source: Pitrè, III, 127.
Eng. *When three watches give the same time,*
That's when Punch will hang himself.
Tr. note: Pitrè remarks that it's unlikely three men will all agree.

Roma Rome.
Roma nun si frabbicau tutta 'ntra un jornu. Source: Pitrè, III, 369.
Eng. *Rome wasn't built in a day.*

ròsuli *n.pl.* chilblain, mild frostbite.
Annu di ròsuli annu d'abbunnanza.
Eng. *A year of chilblain will be a year of abundance.*

rota *n.f.* wheel.
La furtuna è fatta a rota,
Sempri vôta e sbôta. Source: Pitrè, II, 193.
Eng. *Good fortune is like a wheel.*
Always turning in one direction and the other.

rua *n.f.* street, alley, wrinkle.
Ogni rua, un'unza di giudiziu (Chiaramonti). Source: Pitrè, II, 307.
Eng. *Each wrinkle is an ounce of wisdom.*
Tr. note: This proverb is in Pitrè, Volume II, Chapter 43, Youth, Old Age.

Spassu di rua e trìvulu di casa.
Eng. *Entertaining with friends but surly at home.*

rùggia *n.f.* residue, crust of dirt, patina, dregs.
Sta buttigghja è cchjina di rùggia! Source: Piccitto, IV, 265.
Eng. *This bottle is full of dregs!*

Un canùsciri mancu la rùggia. Source: Piccitto, IV, 265.
Eng. *Not knowing anything about anything.*

rùgulu *n.m.* howling, wailing.

A lu rùgulu si conuscinu li lupi. Source: Pitrè, IV, 221.
Eng. *Wolves are recognized by their howling.*

rumpiri *v.t.* break, interrupt.
Cui s'havi a rumpiri lu coddu, trova la scala a lu scuru. Source: Pitrè, II, 270.
Eng. *One who is bent on breaking his neck will manage to find an stairway in the dark.*
Tr. note: This proverb is in Pitrè, Volume II, Chapter 40, Luck.

rusignolu *n.m.* nightingale.
Lu rusignolu vecchiu canta megghiu. Source: Pitrè, II, 306.
Eng. *The old nightingale sings better.*

russània *n.f.* German measles.
La russània havi a vèniri a tutti. Source: Pitrè, IV, 16.
Eng. *German measles will be contracted by all.*
Tr. note: Pitrè explains, because it's reckoned that infants who have not had this skin rash, will have it sooner or later.

russu *adj.* red.
Siddu a la casa armali ha' a tiniri, di pilu russu nè cani nè gatti.
Eng. *If you have to have animals in your house, don't have either a dog or a cat with a red coat.*

Russuliddi *n.m.* red robed clerics.
Quannu la prucissioni è junta a li Russuliddi è signu ch'è spidduta. Source: Pitrè, IV, 255.
Eng. *When the procession reaches the red robed clerics, you know that its near its end.*

ruvettu *n.m.* bush.
Crìscinu li ruvetti
Pri cummigghiari li difetti. Source: Pitrè, I, 36.
Eng. *The bushes grow*
In order to cover defects.
Tr. note: Pitrè notes that this can be understood in other senses, for the most part moral.

rùvulu *n.m.* oak tree.
Lu rùvulu 'un pò fari pira muscareddi. Source: Pitrè, III, 124.

Eng. *An oak doesn't bear muscat pears.*

saccu *n.m.* sack, bag.
Saccu vacanti 'un pó stari a l' addritta. Source: Pitrè, IV, 109.
Eng. *An empty sack cannot stand upright.*

sanari *v.t.* heal, cure.
Lu manciari e lu viviri nni sana,
Chiddu ch' è travagghiari nni cunsuma. Source: Pitrè, III, 205.
Eng. *Eating and drinking heals us;*
It's work that wears us out.
Pitrè notes this is said by those peasants who don't want to work.

Santu Vitu *n.m.* Santu Vitu.
Cui è lu megghiu pò jiri attaccatu a Santu Vitu. Source: Pitrè, I, 210.
Eng. *The best of us can go shackled to St. Vito.*
Pitrè explains: This is a proverb of desperation, that says there is no good person in this world. St. Vito del Capo was an asylum in Palermo, to which wild or crazy people, as considered in those days, were taken, often shackled.

sapienti *adj.* learned, wise.
L'omu chi parra assai, nun dici nenti;
L'omu chi parra picca è sapienti. Source: Pitrè, III, 225.
Eng. *The man who talks a lot, says nothing;*
The man who talks little is wise.

sapiri *v.t.i.* know something, have knowledge.
Contra furtuna nun vali sapìri. Source: Bellantonio, II 192.
Eng. *Knowledge is no match for luck.*

Nun sapemu cui su' li merri e cu' su' li marvizzi. Source: Bellantonio, II 187.
Eng. *We don't know which are the Merli and which the Malvizzi.*
Lit. *It's the equivalent of our saying, We can't tell the one from the other.*
Tr. note: Merli and malvizzi are the names of two types of birds, blackbirds and thrushes. The merri and marvizzi were two sides in a rebellion during 1672-1678. The letters l and r are among those that are often interchanged in various parts of Sicily.

Quantu sai, tantu vai. Source: Pitrè, IV, 46.
Eng. *You're worth as much as you know.*

sarvari *v.t.* save, keep, conserve.
Li dinari sarvati gran guerra fannu. Source: Pitrè, III, 264.
Eng. Turmoil accompanies inheritance.
Lit. Saved money makes for a great war.

sàturu *adj.* full, satiated.
Cu' è saturu schifia.Source: Pitrè, I, 14.
Eng. Once satiated, he scorns.

sautu *n.m.* jump, leap.
Si la jumenta fa lu sautu, la putra lu fa cchiù autu.
Eng. If the mare jumps, the filly will jump higher.

saviu *adj. and n.m.* learned, expert, wise man.
L'omu saviu di pocu si cuntenta. Source: Pitrè, IV, 50.
Eng. The wise man is happy with little.

sàziu *adj.* sated, satisfied.
Megghiu muriri saziu ca dijunu.
Eng. It's better to die sated than hungry.

sbirru *n.m.* cop.
Diu nni scanza di lu sbirru sicilianu e di cchiù quann'è palermitanu!
Eng. God protect us from the Sicilian cop, especially if he's from Palermo.

sbrizza *n.f.* droplet, particle, spurt, spark, splash, tiny bit, fig. pest.
La gatta di lu firraru si caccia li sbrizzi cu la vrancuzza (**Chiaramonte**).
Source: Pitrè, IV, 209.
Eng. The smithy's cat brushes off the droplets with her little paws.
Pitrè notes: "**Vrancuzza**, dim. of **vranca**..."

sbuccia *v.i.* flowers, blooms.
Quannu l'oliva sbuccia 'ntr'aprili, si cogghi cu li varrili;
Quannu l'oliva sbuccia 'ntra giugnu, si cogghi cu lu pugnu. Source: Pitrè, I, 60.
Eng. When the olive trees bloom in April, olives are harvested with barrels,
When they bloom in June, they are harvested in handfuls.

scagghja *n.f.* fish scale, snake slough, canine tooth, wood chips, stone chip, speck, pebble.

Lu figghiu di lu lupu nasci cu li scagghi. Source: Bellantonio, II 155.

Eng. *The wolf's pup is born with fangs.*

Scagghi d' Agustu e acitu di Sittèmmiru. Source: Pitrè, I, 63.

Eng. *Out of food from last year's harvest by August and out of last year's wine by September.*

Lit. *Scraps in August and vinegar in September.*

scaltru *adj.* shrewd, sharp, astute, clever.

C'un paru di gaddini e 'na vivuta

Si sugnu scaltru, accattu la tinuta. Source: Pitrè, I, 43.

Eng. *With a pair of chickens and a drink,*

If I'm clever, I'll buy a holding.

Tr. note: When a latifondia, a land management technique introduced by the Romans, was planted in cereal, it was customary in feudal times, to break the area into manageable territories that would be leased to individual farmers. The farmers would compete to get the best territory by giving the latifondia steward whatever gifts they could manage.

scapulari *v.t.* release the herd, liberate, free.

A lu gridari di li pecuri, scàpula li cani. Source: Bellantonio, II 197.

Eng. *At the bleating of the sheep, release the dogs.*

scarsizza *n.f.* scarcity.

La scarsizza fa lu prezzu. Source: Pitrè, I, 320.

Eng. *Scarcity sets the price.*

Tr. note: This proverb is in Pitrè, Volume I, Chapter 24, Dealing, Commerce.

scausu *adj.* barefoot, unshod horse.

Nun vaja scausu cui simina spini,

Chi poi si punci a la diminticata. Source: Pitrè, II, 373

Eng. *Don't walk barefoot where you've scattered thorns*

For you'll pick up splinters from those you've offended and forgotten.

Tr. note: This proverb is in Pitrè, Volume II, Chapter 50, Insult, Offenses.

sceccu *n.m.* donkey.

Cui campa sceccu, 'un pò mòriri cavaddu. Source: Pitrè, III, 120.

Eng. *He who lives as a donkey can't die as a horse.*

scegghiri *v.t.* choose, select.

Di li dui mali lu menu ti scegghi. Source: Pitrè, III, 291.

Eng. *Choose the lesser of two evils.*

schifiusu *adj.* squeamish, finicky.
Cci su' omini, straòmini, schifiusi e galantomini. Source: Pitrè, III, 120.
Eng. *There are men, extraordinary men, squeamish men, and gentlmen.*

schifu *n.m.* trough, earthenware, huge plate, the smithy's cold water container. Also: **Scifu**
Lu porcu si sonna lu schifu. Source: Pitrè, IV, 210.
Eng. *The pig dreams about the trough.*

sciacqua-lattuchi *n.m.* dumb, foolish.
Cci su' signuri di sciacqua-lattuchi. Source: Pitrè, I, 80.
Eng. *There are noblemen who are foolish.*

sciamu *n.m.* swarm, horde, fig. crowd, multitude, mass.
Sciami di marzu, bon meli ti fazzu.
Eng. *Swarms in March make good honey.*

sciarri *n.f.* fights, squabbles, quarrels.
Quannu li dui nun vonnu, li tri nun si sciarrianu.
Eng. *When two don't want to, three won't quarrel.*

sciddicari *v.i.* slip, slide.
Megghiu sciddicari di pedi chi di lingua Source: Pitrè, III, 228.
Eng. *Better slippery under foot than a slip of the lip.*

Si a carta cadi, tutta a scïenza sciddica. Source: Piccitto, IV, 654.
Eng. *Unable to function without reference to books.*
Lit. *If the paper falls, all knowledge slips.*

scienza *n.f.* science, knowledge. *Also: scïenza, scïènzia.*
L' omu chi di scienza è amaturi, cu lu so tempu si fa onuri. Source: Pitrè, IV, 42.
Eng. *The man who is a lover of science (knowledge) will gain honor in time (himself proud in his own time.)*

scioccu *adj.* silly, stupid, foolish.
Nun pratticari mai cu genti sciocca. Source: Pitrè, III, 327.
Eng. *Never have anything to do with people who are stupid.*

Sciroccu *n.m.* Sirocco.
Di lu Sciroccu e di lu Libbici,
Lu marinaru beni nu nni dici. Source: Pitrè, III, 52.
Eng. The sailor has nothing good to say.
About the Sirocco and the Southwest Wind.

scogghiu *n.m.* rock, submerged rock in the sea.
Un annu si passa supra un scògghiu. Source: Pitrè, III, 250.
Eng. It seems like a year when we're on the rocks.
Lit. A year passes on the rock.
Tr. note: This proverb is in Pitrè, Volume III, Chapter 56, Patience, Resignation.
The Costa Concordia, which went aground off the west coast of Italy on Jan 13,
2012 has been there for more than a year.

scuitari *v.t.i* annoy, disturb, listen, obey.
Cani chi dormi nun scuitari. Source: Pitrè, III, 294.
Eng. Let the sleeping dog lie.

scumitanza *n.f.* uncomfortableness, inconvenience, nuisance.
La scumitanza ogni erruri fa fari. Source: Pitrè, III, 263.
Eng. Nuisances occasion every kind of error.

scupa *n.f.* broom.
Fari vidiri di quali erba si fa la scupa. Source: Moceo, 95..
Eng. Admonish someone.
Lit. Make someone understand from which type of grass the broom is
made.

scupetta *n.f.* rifle, shotgun.
Cui voli fari detta,
Nun va supra l'omini, e si pigghia la scupetta (**Termini**). Source: Pitrè, I,
70.
Eng. If you want to fall into debt
Don't supervise your workers, take your shotgun and go off hunting.

scurdari *v.t.* forget.
Cui vasa 'na vucca, si nni scorda 'n' àutra. Source: Pitrè, I, 16.
Eng. He who kisses one mouth, forgets the other one.

scurtillari *v.t.* upstage, excoriate, criticize. *Also: scorticare, scurcillata.*
A maistru scurtillari? Source: Pitrè, IV, 235.

Eng. Would you upstage the master?

sdignari *v.t.* despise, provoke disdain.
Tutti cosi vennu a sdegnanu, lu pani 'un sdegna mai. Source: Pitrè, IV, 111.
Eng. Everything comes to be despised, but bread is never despised.

sdiri *v.t.* retract.
Lu diri e lu sdiri è sapienza. Source: Pitrè, III, 185.
Eng. Saying and retracting is wisdom.

sdivacari *v.t.* empty.
Vôi sdivacari tutta la cannata?
Carduni amaru, e favuzza caliata. Source: Pitrè, IV, 112.
Eng. Do you want to empty the jug?
Eat bitter cardoons and roasted broad beans.

sedda *n.f.* saddle.
A bon cavaddu nun cci manca sedda. Source: Pitrè, III, 188.
Eng. A saddle is always available for a good horse.

sèdiri *v.i.* sit, situate.
Cui beni sedi, nun si mova. Source: Pitrè, IV, 225.
Eng. Who is well situated, stays put.

segretu *n.m.* secret.
Cu' lu segretu a la sua donna fida, nni farà pubblica grida.
Eng. If you confide a secret to your woman, you'll make it public knowledge.

sennu *n.m.* judgement, good sense.
A testa bianca spissu lu sennu manca.
Eng. There's no fool like an old fool.
Lit. The white head often lacks good sense.

sepurtura *n.f.* grave.
Lu vinu fa figura:
Fa nèsciri l'omu di la sepurtura. Source: Pitrè, IV, 141.
Eng. Wine is empowering:
It lets a man leave the grave.

serenità *n.f.* serenity, tranquility.
A tri cosi creditu nun dati; serenità d'invernu e nuvuli di stati, amuri di donna, e carità di frati, l'unu e l'autru nun sunnu custanti.
Eng. *There are three things you shouldn't give credence to: a calm winter, clouds in summer, the love of women, and the charity of friars.*

serpi *n.f.* snake, serpent.
Li cosi longhi addiventanu serpi. Source: Pitrè, III, 378.
Eng. Matters not quicklt resolved, fester.
Lit. *Long things become snakes.*
Tr. note: This proverb is in Pitrè, Volume III, Chapter 74, Resoluteness, Solicitude, Seize the Opportunity.

Ogni serpi havi lu sò vilenu. Source: Pitrè, 1, 269.
Eng. *Every snake has its own venom.*

seru *n.m.* serum.
Lu seru arrifresca. Source: Pitrè, IV, 21.
Eng. *The serum purges.*
Tr. note: Pitrè, besides being an eminent folklorist, was also a practicing medical doctor. That might explain this note following this proverb, "Namely purgative, because the common folk say ***refresh*** and ***purge*** interchangeably. There is also this sentence from the Salerno School: Inciditque, lavat, penetrat, mundat quoque serum."
Therefore, Pitrè is relying on his medical background to interpret *seru* to mean laxative since he has observed that the people use the terms ***refresh*** and ***purge*** interchangeably.

serviri *v.t. and v.i.* serve, be useful.
Quann' hai l'occasioni servitinni. Source: Pitrè, III, 373.
Eng. *When you're given an advantage, take it.*

servu *n.m.* servant, waiter, domestic.
Li servi su' nemici salariati: cchiù chi li trasi dintra, cchiu nèscinu fora.
Source: Pitrè, IV, 244.
Eng. *Servants are salaried enemies: the more you have, the more you lose.*

settembri *n.m.* September.
Quannu in settembri cauru e asciuttu domina, la terra si prepara pri la semina.
Eng. *When September is hot and dry, prepare the soil for seeding.*

sfari *v.t.* undo, waste, kill.
Cui fici lu munnu, lu pò sfari. Source: Pitrè, IV, 180.
Eng. God giveth and God taketh away.

sfilazza *n.f.* a draft from a crack in a wall, window, or door.
Megghiu friscu di chiazza
Ca friscu di sfilazza. Source: Pitrè, IV, 23.
Eng. Better the fresh air from the square,
Than the draft from a crack.

Megghiu vastuniatu ccu na mazza ca ventu di sfilazza.
Eng. Better a beating with a mallet than a draft through a crack.

sfilòcchi *n.m.* unravelling threads.
Diu nni scanza di divirtirinni cu li sfilòcchi di la cutra e cu la lana di li chiumazza. Source: Pitrè, Vol, Page.
Eng. Lord save us from entertaining ourselves with unravelling blanket threads and pillow wool.

sfrazziari *v.i.* spend freely, show off.
Megghiu muriri sfrazziannu, chi campari addisiannu. Source: Pitrè, III, 272.
Eng. It's better to die as a spendthrift than to live a life of want.

sfrinatu *adj.* dissolute, profligate, debauched.
Pri lu tantu curriri sfrinatu,
Cascavi e nun mi pozzu dari ajutu (*Catania*). Source: Pitrè, IV, 119.
Eng. On account of my running uncontrollably I fell and can't help myself.

sgarrari *v.t.* err, sin, go astray, mistake, miss.
Cosa sgarrata, menza 'nzirtata. Source: Pitrè, II, 168.
Eng. An error made, learning started.

sgarruni *n.m.* enormous mistake.
Diu ti scansi di sgarruni di granni. Source: Pitrè, IV, 11.
Eng. May God protect you from the mistakes of powerful men.

sgravari *v.t.* alleviate, lighten.
Li multi manu sgravanu travagghiu. Source: Pitrè, III, 203.
Eng. Many hands make light work.

si *refl.pron.* self.
Nuddu si lamenta si nun si doli. Source: Pitrè, II. 181.
Eng. No one complains if he is not hurting.

siari *v.i.* be, being, existence.
Mentri avemu, semu vuluti;
Quannu 'un avemu, addiu siati. Source: Pitrè, III, 272.
Eng. While we have, we are welcomed;
When we don't have, we cease to exist.
Lit. When we have, we are wanted;
When we don't have, good bye.
Tr. note: This proverb is in Pitrè, Volume III, Chapter 67, Poverty, Wealth.

siccari *v.i.* dry up.
Cchiù chi su', fannu cchiù assai,
Ma la panza nun si jinchi mai,
E la vurza 'nsicchirai (**Castelvetrano**). Source: Pitrè, IV, 211.
Eng. The more there are, the more gets done,
But the stomach never fills up,
And the purse dries up.

Sicilia *place name* Sicily.
'N Sicilia sànanu li testi rutti, ma no li gammi malati. Source: Pitrè, IV, 26.
Eng. Sicily cures the soul but not the body.
Lit. In Sicily broken heads are cured, but not sick legs.
Tr. note: Pitrè, always the doctor, adds, "Those legs, according to an opinion of our good, ancient doctors, could be cured in Naples."

Pri sùrfaru, frummentu, vini e lani, viniti di Sicilia a li paisi.
Eng. For sulphur, wheat, wine, and wool, come to the towns and villages of Sicily.

sicilianu *adj.* Sicilian.
Cavaddu sicilianu: curtu e nanu. Source: Pitrè, I, 124.
Eng. The Sicilian horse: short and dwarfish.
Pitrè adds: "Sono i caratteri della razza cavallina di Sicilia."
Eng. These are the characteristics of the Sicilian breed of horses.

sicutari *v.t.* follow, continue, proceed.
Lu stissu sicutari è migghiuria. Source: Pitrè, IV, 22.
Eng. Perseverance is the same as betterment.

Sgarrari è di l'omini, lu sicutari è di li bestii. Source: Pitrè, III, 185.
Eng. *To err is human, to err repeatedly is beastly.*

siddiari *v.t.* annoy, bother, torment.
Sempri 'na cosa siddia. Source: Pitrè, IV, 254.
Eng. *Always doing the same thing is tedious.*

siggillu *n.m.* symbol, seal, impression
Lu siggillu di l'omu dabbeni è la parola. Source: Pitrè, III, 283.
Eng. *The sign of a man's decency is his word.*

signa *n.f.* monkey, homely woman, mantis.
Anchi a la signa cci piaci lu duci. Source: Pitrè, I, 12.
Eng. *Even the monkey likes sweets.*

La signa binchì si vesti di sita, sempri è signa. Source: Pitrè, IV, 131.
Eng. *A monkey, though it dresses in silk, is still a monkey.*

signu *n.m.* sign, proof.
Quannu lu riccu parra cu lu poviru, è signu chi nn'havi di bisognu. Source: Pitrè, III, 275.
Eng. *When the rich man talks with the poor man, it's a sign that he needs something.*

Signuri *n.m.* Lord, God.
Lu Signuri joca gravusu, ma è sempri patri misiricurdiusu.
Eng. *God plays seriously, but He's always a merciful father.*

signuri *n.m.* lord, gentleman, boss, master, owner.
A gran signuri picculu prisenti. Source: Pitrè, I, 79.
Eng. *A small gift for a powerful master.*
Tr. note: The proverb is derived from the short story of the same name in Pitrè, IV, 333.

A lu tò signuri ed a lu Rè,
Bisogna mantinirci la fè. Source: Pitrè, I, 79.
Eng. *You have to keep faith,*
In your master and your King.
Tr. note: Pitrè adds that he has never heard this proverb, but that it is in the collection by Catania.

signurìa *n.f.* nobility, elegance, power, arrogance.
Amuri e signurìa nun vonnu cumpagnia. Source: Pitrè, I, 104.
Eng. Love and arrogance don't want company.

simenza *n.f.* seed.
Cu sciloccu jetta simenza, cu tramuntana no.
Eng. Sow with the Sirocco but not with the North Wind.

siminari *v.t.* sow, seed, inseminate.
A Sant' Andria lu bonu massaru siminatu avia.
Eng. The good steward has planted by St. Andrew's Day. (November 30).

Simuni *n.m.* Simon
Pri San Simuni e Giura
Li nèspuli s'appènninu a lu mura. Source: Pitrè, III, 50.
Eng. On the feast of Saints Simon and Jude (Oct. 28),
The fruit of the medlar tree are hung on the wall to ripen.

sinnacu *n.m.* mayor.
Lu Sinnacu cci dissi a li bagasci: Pigghiàtivi 'u tempu comu veni. Source:
Pitrè, III, 246.
Eng. The mayor said to the prostitutes: You need to accept the times as
they are.
Note: Pitrè explains that this proverb came from a new law that was passed limiting
the activity of prostitutes and requiring them to wear a yellow ribbon in their hair.
About twenty of them went to the mayor to have him ask the king to repeal the
new law. He told them he couldn't do that. He said they should go to the king
themselves. They said if they went to the king, he would kill them. And the mayor
answered that they need to accept the times as they are.

sintimentu *n.m.* sentiment, feeling, tact, respect, sense, judgement.
Tanti omini, tanti sintimenti. Source: Pitrè, III, 127.
Eng. Many men, many views.

sìpali *n.m.* live hedge, small wall around a small farm.
Li sipàli non hannu occhi e vidinu, li mura non hannu aricchi e sèntunu
(*Catania*). Source: Pitrè, IV, 165.
Eng. The hedges have no eyes, and they see; the walls have no ears, and
they hear.

sira *n.f.* evening.

Lu manciari di la sira è persu. Source: Pitrè, IV, 97.
Eng. Eating in the evening is wasted.

sirenu *n.f.* dew. *Also: risena.*
Sirenu nun jinchi jisterni.
Eng. Dew doesn't fill the cisterns.

siritina *n.f.* evening, night.
Quannu la siritina è mala,
Pigghia pri la retina la mula. Source: Pitrè, III, 296.
Eng. When the night is bad,
Take the mule by the bridle.

sirpenti *n.m.* serpent.
Megghiu 'mmucca di un sirpenti,
Ca 'mmucca di li mali genti. Source: Pitrè, II, 403.
Eng. Better the mouth of a serpent,
Than the mouthings of the malicious.

sirvizziu *n.m.* service.
Gran sirviziu veni spissu pagatu d' ingratitutini.
Eng. A great service is often paid with ingratitude.

Sirvizziu fattu, mircedi aspetta.
Eng. Service rendered; payment awaited.

sita *n.f.* silk.
Si nun pòi purtari la sita porta la lana. Source: Piccitto, II, 429.
Eng. Do the best you can.
Lit. If you can't bring silk, bring wool.

sittembri *n.m.* September.
Ghianna ed oliva, a sittembri si vidi.
Eng. September brings acorns and olives.

sittèmmiru *n.m.* September.
Agustu cucina e sittèmmiru minestra. Source: Pitrè, III, 5.
Eng. In August, cook, in September, soup.
Tr. note: Pitrè cites the ancient custom in Sicily for tenant farmers to move after the end of August and start renting anew in September.

smargiazzu *n.m.* braggart, boaster.
Li smargiazzi su' comu li campani, chi chiamanu genti, ed iddi sempri stannu fora. Source: Pitrè, III, 241.
Eng. *Braggarts are like the bells that call people while they always remain outside.*

smizzigghjari *v.t.* to spoil, coddle excessively.
Figghiu smizzighiatu è malu criatu. Source: Bellantonio, II 148.
Eng. *A spoiled son is ill prepared for life.*

sò *pos. pron.* his, hers, its, their.
Ogni firita havi cu idda lu sò duluri. Source: Pitrè, IV, 27.
Eng. *Every wound comes with its own pain.*

sòggira *n.f.* mother-in-law.
La sòggira nun è mancu bona di zuccaru
Eng. *The mother-in-law isn't good even she is made of sugar.*

Qual'è chidda nora chi voli beniri a la sòggira.
Eng. *Show me the daughter-in-law who likes her mother-in-law.*

sòi *pos. pron.* his own.

Ognunu cu li soi.
Eng. *Each with his own.*

sona *v.t.* plays.
Lu picciottu sona lu flautu, l'uomu di menza aità sona lu cìmmalu, e lu viecciu sona l' organu (**Modica**). Source: Pitrè, II, 305.
Eng. *The young man plays the flute, the middle aged man plays the harpsichord, the old man plays the organ.*
Tr. note: This proverb is in Pitrè, Volume II, Chapter 43, Youth, Old Age.

Sona a chidda parti unni ti tocca. Source: Pitrè, III, 330.
Eng. *Play in those places where you will entertain.*
Pitrè adds:
"Si vox est, canta, si mollia brachia salta,
Et quacumque potes dote placere, place." Ovid.
If you have a voice, sing; if your limbs are supple, dance,
And thus give pleasure by whatever means. Ovid.

sonnu *n.m.* sleep, dream.
Lu sonnu di la notti cunsigghia l'omu. Source: Pitrè, II, 289.
Eng. *Sleep is the best meditation. (Thomas Jefferson)*
Lit. *The sleep of night counsels man.*
Tr. note: This proverb is in Pitrè, Volume II, Chapter 42, Day, Night.

sonu *n.m.* sound, tone, music.
A lu sonu si canusci la compana.
Eng. *The bell is recognized by its ring.*

spadda *n.f.* shoulder, back.
Li megghiu parenti su li spaddi. Source: Bellantonio, II 154.
Eng. *Self help is your best relative.*
Lit. *The best relatives are the shoulders.*

Mussu di purceddu, oricchi di mircanti e spaddi d'asineddu.
Eng. *Look into everything, believe nothing, bear any burden.*
Lit. *The snout of a piglet, the ears of a merchant, and the back of a donkey.*

spagghiari *v.t.* winnow, scatter, waste, squander.
Mannari a spagghiari l'acqua.
Eng. *To send on a fool's errand.*
Lit. *To send to winnow water.*

spaiàri *v.t.* loosen, untie, free oxen from the yoke.
Quannu chjova a mmenzê matina pigghj'a coffa e bbassimina,
Quannu chjova ri vèspir'e nnotti spàiê vòi e stài ê bbotti. Source: Piccitto,
V, 113.
Eng. *When it rains in the morning take your lunch basket and go do the*
seeding,
When it rains between vespers and the night, free the oxen and put aside
your boots.

spànniri *v.t.* spread, expand, stretch, distribute, shed.
Lu saccu di chi è china, spanni. Source: Pitrè, III, 124.
Eng. *The sack leaks of whatever it is full.*

sparagnari *v.t.* conserve, save, spare.
Li robbi vecchi sparagnanu li novi. Source: Pitrè, IV, 131.
Eng. *Old clothes conserve the new.*
Pitrè notes that this particular proverb may also be listed in the Chapter on Economy, which is in Volume II. Pitrè organized his collection of some 13,000 proverbs into ninety Chapters, grouped by subject and alphabetized by the first word of the chapter title. I chose to organize my English translation by keyword because my primary interest is to make the Sicilian vocabulary accessible to English speakers, letting the content of the proverb serve as an example of the use of the keyword.

sparagnu *n.m.* saving, savings.
Lu sparagnu è lu primu guadagnu.
Eng. *A penny saved, is a penny earned.*
Lit. *Saving is the first earning.*

spassari *v.i.* entertain oneself.
Cui si spassa picciottu, rèpita vecchiu. Source: Bellantonio, II, 210.
Eng. *Who lives foolishly as a youth, wails in old age.*

spata *n.f.* sabre, sword.
Cchiù nn'ammazza la gula chi la spata. Source: Pitrè, IV, 4.
Eng. *Gluttony kills more people than die by the sword.*
Note. Pitrè quotes Cicero, Plures enim videmus gula quam gladio cadere.

spatuliaturi *n.m.* hackler, flax or hemp comber.
Tri sunnu li nnimici di lu latru: la luna, li cani e li spatuliaturi. Source:
Pitrè, II, 285.
Eng. *Three are the enemies of the thief: the moon, dogs, and hacklers.*

Tr. note: Pitrè explains that hacklers customarily did their work of combing the fibers of flax or hemp at night, and in the middle of the street, that's why, like the light of the moon and dogs, hacklers were a hindrance to would be robbers.

spavintari *v.t.* frighten, terrify, scare.
Pri li spaventi, vennu l'accidenti. Source: Pitrè, III, 243.
Eng. *From fears come accidents.*

speddiri *v.i.t.* to cease, to finish.
Cu' speddi prima ajuta lu cumpagnu.
Eng. *The one who finishes first helps his companion.*

spènniri *v.t.* to spend.
Cu' cchiù spenni menu spenni. Source: Pitrè, I, 314.
Eng. *Who buys quality spends less.*

spezziu *n.m.* pepper, spices.
Li spèzzii tràsinu a tutti banni, Source: Pitrè, IV, 95.
Eng. *Spices are used in everything.*

spiculari *v.t.i.* glean, gather; speculate, consider, deliberate, think.
L'omu, finu a la morti specula. Source: Pitrè, IV, 182.
Eng. *Man speculates until his death.*
Pitrè adds: "So as to inform or direct his actions."

spirari *v.t.i.* hope, expect.
Cui spera nna lu monacu, spera ricògghiri lu ventu 'ntra la riti.
Eng. *Putting hope in a monk is like hoping to catch the wind in a net.*

spirdatu *adj.* possessed, fanatical.
A un populu mattu, un parrinu spirdatu. Source: Pitrè, IV, 160.
Eng. *For a crazy people, a priest who is possessed.*

Spirlinga *place name* Sperlinga.
Sola Sperlinga negavit. Source: Pitrè, III, 168.
Eng. *Only Sperlinga demurred.*

Spirlinga nigò. Source: Pitrè, III, 168-9.
Eng. *Sperlinga said no.*
Pitrè cites Michele Amari and his book on The War of the Sicilian Vespers, Vol. 1, Ch VI and includes a long quotation in which Amari maintains that the French

who were able to resist for over a year in the castle at Sperlinga, had the help of the local population. It's further posited that the brevity of the proverb is designed to discourage the perpetuation of an unpleasant memory and to obscure the shameful incident from foreigners.

squartari *v.t.* quartered, divided in four.
Megghiu 'mpisu ca squartatu. Source: Pitrè, III, 293.
Eng. *Better the lesser of two evils.*
Lit. *Better hanged than quartered.*

staffa *n.f.* stirrup.
Stari cu lu pedi alla staffa.
Eng. *To be ready.*
Lit. *To be with your feet in the stirrups.*

stafferi *n.m.* groom, servant.
Cu' havi manu e pedi,
Nun ha bisognu di stafferi. Source: Pitrè, III, 194.
Eng. *He who has hands and feet*
Has no need for a servant.

stanchizza *n.f.* fatigue, weariness.
Lu guadagnu fa passari la stanchizza. Source: Pitrè, II, 355.
Eng. *Earnings make weariness pass.*

stari *v.i.* live, be, stay, persevere.
Chiddu è lu bonu stari, unni è lu bonu campari.
Eng. *It's a good place to stay, where you can make a good living.*

stati *n.f.* summer, state, country.
Una bedda jurnata nun fa stati. Source: Pitrè, IV, 191.
Eng. *One fine day does not a summer make.*

stenta *n.m.* distress, privation, need, pain.
Sempri stenta cu' mai è cuntenta. Source: Pitrè, I, 306.
Eng. *One who is never satisfied is always in need.*

stigghiu *n.m.* implement, tool.
Ogni diavulu travagghia cu li so' stigghi. Source: Pitrè, IV, 245.
Eng. *Every master craftsman works with his own tools.*
Pitrè adds: "***Diavulu***, qui ***maestro***; ***stigghi***, **arnesi**, strumenti, ferri ecc." Eng. ***Devil***,

here means *master*; *stigghi*, are *tools.*

stimari *v.t.* esteem, admire, regard, respect, value.
Cu' havi dinari ed amicizia,
Pocu stima la giustizia. Source: Pitrè, II, 319.
Eng. People with money and friends
Have little regard for justice.
Tr. note: This proverb is in Pitrè, Volume II, Chapter 45, Justice, Litigation.

stipa *n.f.* cask, very large, 800-1600 liters
La bona stipa fa bonu vinu. Source: Pitrè, IV, 137.
Eng. A good cask makes good wine.

stizza *n.f.* a drop of any liquid, a rain drop.
Livarisi di li stizzi e mittirisi a li canali.
Eng. Going from bad to worse.
Lit. Avoiding the dripping and going into the canal.

stranutari *v.i.* sneeze.
Quannu lu tempu si muta, la vèstia stranuta. Source: Pitrè, III, 56.
Eng. When the weather changes, the beast sneezes.

strasiccu *adj.* very dry.
Oriu strasiccu, e lavuri bruciareddu. Source: Pitrè, I, 56.
Eng. Barley that's dried and wheat that has not matured perfectly.
Pitrè explains that the harvest time of barley is not critical, but not so for wheat, which must be harvested on time.

strata *n.f.* street, road, fig. headway.
Tutt' i strati nèsciun' a marina.
Eng. All roads lead to the sea.
Tr. note. This is the island's equivalent of the mainland's, *All roads lead to Rome.*

stravisari *v.t.* distort, alter, scar, waste, break, mistreat.
Roggiu, citarra e scupetta
Stravìsanu la sacchetta (*Alimena*). Source: Pitrè, II, 152.
Eng. A watch, a guitar, and a shotgun
Break the purse.
Tr. note: Pitrè has a long three paragraph explanation of this proverb. A watch always needs repair of one sort or another, ammunition for the shotgun requires powder, wadding and pellets, and the guitar means dancing and partying and wasting time.

All the above being a drain on the wallet.

strizzari *v.t.* comb out a braid.
Mmaliditta chidda trizza,
Chi di Vènnari si strizza;
Biniditta chidda pasta,
Chi di Vènnari si 'mpasta. Source: Pitrè, III, 346.
Eng. *Accursed is she with braids,*
Who combs them out on Friday;
Blessed is she who kneads
Who does the kneading on Friday.
Note: Pitrè explains that this proverb is about a traveler who is given a requested drink of water by a woman who was kneading dough, after being refused by a woman who was combing out her braids.

struppiàtu *adj.* hurt, wounded, crippled.
Pri lu jornu di Sant'Agàta (5 Febbr.)
Figghianu li ciunchi e struppiati. Source: Pitrè, III, 49.
Eng. *For the day of Saint Agatha (Feb. 5)*
The lame and crippled hens lay eggs.

stuppa *n.f.* Course or waste flax prepared for spinning, tow, oakum.
Quannu ti cridi d'aviri ventu 'n puppa, tannu ti trovi la varva di stuppa.
Eng. *When you think you have the wind at your back, that's when you'll be disappointed.*

stuzzicari *v.t.* poke, prod.
Stuzzicari lu cani chi dormi.
Eng. *Inviting trouble.*

Nun stuzzicari lu cani chi dormi. Source: Pitrè, III, 294.
Eng. *Don't prod a sleeping dog.*

succedi *v.i.* happen.
Vôi sapiri chi succedi?
Va nni mònachi e varveri. Source: Pitrè, IV, 385.
Eng. *To know what's happening,*
Go to the monasteries and barbershops.

sucu *n.m.* juice, gravy, sip; essence.
Cui pò tirari sucu di 'na petra? Source: Pitrè, III, 259.

Eng. *You can't squeeze blood out of a stone.*
Lit. *He who can pull juice out of a stone?*

suda *v.i.* . Sweat, perspire.
A santu chi nun suda nun ti cci addinucchiari. Source: Pitrè, II, 350.
Eng. *Don't kneel in front of a saint who doesn't perspire.*

suffriri *v.t. and v.i.* To bear, to endure, to suffer.
Bisogna suffriri lu statu prisenti, pri nun aviri lu mali avviniri. Source:
Pitrè, III, 247.
Eng. *Put up with your present condition to avoid a bad future.*

suggizioni *n.f.* subjection, uneasiness, apprehension, fear. Fear
Unni nun cc' è suggizioni, nun cc' è nè re, nè raggiuni. Source: Pitrè, I, 86.
Eng. *Where there is not subjection, there is neither a king, nor reason.*
It is the thinking expressed in this proverb, that without a king you have anarchy,
that led the Sicilian barons, to ask Peter of Aragon for help. This brought to a quick
end the self government the Sicilians had achieved with their victory in 1282. Less
than a year after taking over, Peter of Aragon quashed any lingering aspirations
for Sicilian independence by having Gualtiero di Caltagirone, one of the leaders
of the movement for independence, publically decapitated in piazza San Giuliano
on May 22, 1283.

suli *n.m.* sun.
Agurari lu suli chi affaccia.
Eng. *Welcome the help that arrives.*
Lit. *Welcome the sun that comes out.*

suliri *v.i.* be usual, be normal.
Cu' ti fa zoccu nun ti soli, o ti ha gabbatu, o gabbari ti voli.
Eng. *Who does the unusual is either planning to or has already deceived*
you.

sulitariu *n.m.* a sparrow of this name.
Quannu arrinesci un minciuni, va chiù assai d'un sulitariu (***Noto***). Source:
Pitrè, IV, 46.
Eng. *When a fool succeeds, it's worth more than a sparrow.*
Tr. note: Pitrè says that sulitariu is a sparrow of this name. The Sicilian spelling
of the proverb is in the parrata of Noto, a beautiful baroque city south of Siracusa.

sulu *adj.* alone, without equal, singly.

Binidittu sia ddu malannu chi veni sulu. Source: Pitrè, III, 96.
Eng. Blessed be the bad year that comes by itself.

Quannu veni sula, faciticci la bona facci. Source: Pitrè, III, 96.
Eng. When misfortune comes alone, smile.
Tr. note: This proverb is in Pitrè's Chapter 56 on *Life's Misfortunes, and The Human Condition.*

sumeri *n.m.* donkey, jackass, dunce.
'Ntra maritu e 'ntra mugghieri
Cui si 'mmisca è un gran sumeri. Source: Pitrè, II, 224.
*Eng. Whoever interferes between husband and wife
Is a big jackass.*

sunari *v.t.* ring, play, sound.
Cui mancia babbaluci e vivi acqua,
Sunàti li campani pirchì è mortu. Source: Pitrè, IV, 87.
*Eng. Who eats snails and drinks water,
Ring the church bells for he is dead.*

superbia *n.f.* pride, arrogance.
La superbia è figghia di l'ignoranza.
Eng. Arrogance is the child of ignorance.

superchiu *n.m.* excessive; *adv.* too much, enough.
Superchia curtisia,
Fa dubbitari chi 'ngannu sia. Source: Pitrè,IV, 71.
*Eng. Excessive graciousness
Raises concern that you're being deceitful.*
supirari *v.t..* overcome, surpass, outlast.
Supira lu putiri a lu sapiri. Source: Traina, 787.
Eng. Power trumps knowledge.

Supira lu putiri e lu sapiri. Source: Pitrè, IV, 47.
Eng. Power and knowledge surpass.
Tr. note: Notice the difference in meaning between the Pitrè version and the Traina version.

suppurtari *v.t.* endure, go through.
Bisogna suppurtari lu mali cui voli lu beni. Source: Pitrè, III, 247.

Eng. *You need to endure the bad to enjoy the good.*

supracarta *n.f.* envelope address, envelope, paperweight.
La facci è supracarta di lu cori. Source: Pitrè, III, 298.
Eng. *The face shows what's written on the heart.*

supraniari *v.t..* overcome, win, take advantage, dominate.
Amaru a cui si fa supraniari!
Lustru di paradisu nun ni vidi. Source: Cipolla, 20.
Eng. *Woe to him who lets himself be stepped upon.*
He will never see the light of paradise. Trans by Cipolla.

surci *n.m.* mouse, mice.
Gattu di fàuda 'un pigghia surci. Source: Pitrè, IV, 378.
Eng. *A coddled cat doesn't catch mice.*

surcu *n.m* furrow.
Li pagghiara di lu lavuri sunnu li surchi.
Eng. *The furrows are shelters for the seedlings.*

surdatu *n.m.* soldier.
A bon surdatu si duna bona lancia.
Eng. *The good weapon goes to the capable soldier.*

surdu *adj. and n.m.* deaf.
A ciumi surdi nun cci iri a piscari.
Eng. *Don't deal with a person who is uncommunicative.*
Lit. *Don't fish in a river that's silent.*

surella *n.f.* sister. *Also: soru, sorella.*
Li vucchi su' surelli. Source: Pitrè, I, 20.
Eng. *Mouths are sisters.*

susiri *v.t. refl. .* get up.
Cui si susìu, locu pirdìu; cui s'assittau, locu truvau.
Eng. *Stay put and get organized.*
Lit. *Who got up, lost his place; who sat down, found it.*

suspettu *n.m.* doubt, distrust.
Cu' è di l'arti, è suspettu. Source: Pitrè, IV, 244.

Eng. One who is artsy is distrusted.

suspirari *v.i.* sigh.
Cui suspira 'un è cuntenti, cui santìa 'un havi dinari, cui di vecchi si 'nnamura, si la chianci la vintura.Source: Pitrè, I, 15.
Eng. One who sighs is not content, who curses has no money, whoever falls in love with old men will meet with bad luck.

sustu *n.m.* nuisance, annoyance.
Agustu, lu càudu è sustu. Source: Pitrè, III, 6.
Eng. August, the heat is a nuisance.

susu *adv.* above, on the top floor, on the highest part.
Quannu veni di susu,
Va 'nfilati 'ntra un pirtusu. Source: Pitrè, III, 57.
Eng. When the wind comes from above.
Go find a hole to hide in.

sutta *prep.* under.
Sutt'acqua fami, sutta nivi pani. Source: Pitrè, III, 69.
Eng. Good irrigation gives healthy crops.
Lit. Flooded fields, hunger, snow melt, bread
To explain this proverb, Pitrè includes a quotation from Cuppari who compares the effect on crops of an excessively wet winter versus a snowy winter which turns out to be mostly dry and cold. The natural melting of snow irrigates the field without washing away the topsoil.

suttili *adj* thin, subtle, crisp, keen, sharp, delicate.
Lu viddanu havi aviri scarpi grossi, e ciriveddi suttili.
Eng. The peasant needs big shoes and a sharp mind.

suttirrari *v.t.* bury, inter, oppress, degrade.
Nuddu si pò chiamari biatu,
Avanti chi sia suttirratu. Source: Pitrè, III, 306.
Eng. No one can be called blessed
Before he is burried.

suverchiu *adj.* excessive, superfluous, too much.
Lu picca abbasta, l'assai suverchiu.
Eng. A little is enough, a lot is too much.

tabbacchera *n.f.* snuffbox, very small house, spinning top, female genitals, sweet and flavorful flat fish.
Spitali, spiziaria e galera
Nun nèsciri tabbacchera. Source: Pitrè, IV, 177.
Eng. *In a hospital, a pharmacy, and a jail*
Don't take out a snuffbox.
Pitrè adds: "because they'll quickly empty it."

tabbaccu *n.m.* tobacco
Lu vinu, lu tabbaccu e li donni ruinanu l' omu. Source: Pitrè, IV, 148.
Eng. *Wine, tobacco, and women are man's ruination.*

tacca *n.f.* stain, soil, spot, blemish.
All'oru nun cci pò tacca, e mancu a fodedda nova cci vali pezza. Source: Pitrè, III, 279.
Eng. *Don't besmirch the reputation of an honorable man.*
Lit. *You can't soil gold, nor should you patch a new gown.*

tacchiari *v.t.* soil, stain, mar, dirty.
Supra l'oru nun cci pò tacca. Source: Pitrè, III, 286.
Eng. *Gold can't be soiled.*

Supra niura nun cci pò tacca. Source: Pitrè, III, 286.
Eng. *You can't shame the wicked.*
Lit. *You can't dirty on black.*

taciri *v.i.* be silent, to not speak.
Assai sa, cui sa, si taciri sa. Source: Pitrè, III, 215.
Eng. *He is wise who knows to be silent.*

Assai sapi cui taciri sapi. Source: Pitrè, III, 215.
Eng. *He is wise who knows to be silent.*

È megghiu taciri ca malu parrari.
Eng. *It's better to be silent than to speak badly.*

La gaddina si tacissi
Quannu fa l'ovu 'un si sapissi. Source: Pitrè, III, 221.
Eng. *If the hen remained silent,*
When she lays an egg no one would know.

Lu taciri è risposta e lu finciri è curtisia. Source: Pitrè, III, 227.
Eng. *Silence is a reply, and pretence is a courtesy.*

Lu tàciri è virtù ma 'un è di tutti,
E lu dari risposta è 'na bell'arti;
E si si duna risposta a tutti,
Si perdi sennu, virtuti ed arti. Source: Pitrè, III, 227.
Eng. *Silence is a virtue, but it's not universally shared,*
And replying is a fine art;
And if a reply is given to all,
Lost are judgement, virtue and art.
Note: Pitrè provides references to Ariosto, Orl. fur., VII, 30, Euripedes and Proverbs
XVII, 28: Even a fool, when he holdeth his peace, is counted wise: and he that
shutteth his lips is esteemed a man of understanding.

Vidi e taci si beni aviri voi o si vo' campari 'm paci.
Eng. *Observe and be silent if you want to live well or live in peace.*

taddarita *n.f.* agitated, bat, cloak.
'Mmatula, taddarita, canti e soni,
Lu santu ch'è di màrmuru nun suda. Source: Pitrè, III, 186.
Eng. *The situation is hopeless.*
Lit. *Being agitated, singing and making music are useless,*
The saint that's made of marble doesn't perspire.

tagghiari *v.t.* cut, trim, prune.
Arvulu chi nun fa fruttu, tagghialu di li radici. Source: Bonner, 101.
Eng. *A tree that doesn't bear fruit, cut it at its roots.*
Meaning: Get rid of someone (or something) that's no good. Eng. trans.
by Bonner, 101.
'Ntra lu minimu di la luna, e cu ventu tramuntana, tagghia castagni e cersi
(***Madonie***). Source: Pitrè, I, 54.
Eng. *Pick the chestnuts and acorns with the waning of the moon and a*
north wind.

Quannu lu porcu è grassu, sempri cc' è di tagghiari. Source: Bellantonio,
II, 108.
Eng. *With the fattened pig there is always more you can eat.*

tàju *n.m.* mud, adobe, mortar.
Quannu chiovi e nun fa taju,

La Pasqua nun veni 'ntra Maju. Source: Pitrè, III, 53.
Eng. *When it rains but doesn't result in mud,*
Easter won't occur in May.

tali *adj.* like, similar.
A tali pruposta, sia tali risposta. Source: Pitrè, III, 233.
Eng. *Ask a stupid question, get a stupid answer.*

Tali ammazza cui campa 'n paura. Source: Pitrè, III, 243.
Eng. *Whistling in the dark.*
Lit. *Thus one kills who lives in fear.*

taliari *v.t.* look, watch, admire.
Cu' havi occhi, talìa. Source: Pitrè, IV, 180.
Eng. *He who has eyes looks.*

Pignata taliata 'un vugghi mai. Source: Pitrè, IV, 107.
Eng. *A watched pot never boils.*

tampi *neg. particle.* nothing.
Cu' simina 'ntra li timpi, ricogghi tampi.Source: Pitrè, I, 40.
Eng. *Who plants on steep slopes harvests nothing.*
Tr. note: Pitrè explains that tampi is a nonexistent word used for assonance. Both Traina and Piccitto define tampi as a negative particle and Piccitto cites this proverb, while Traina, who often cites proverbs does not cite this one. What the Dickens! It would appear that the author of this proverb invented a new Sicilian word.

tammureddu *n.m.* tambourine.
Criva novi e tammureddi pri tri ghiorna sunnu beddi.
Eng. *Nothing lasts forever.*
Lit. *A new sieve and tambourines are like new for three days.*

Tammureddi e ziti
Tri jorna si vidinu puliti. Source: Pitrè, IV, 233.
Eng. *Tambourines and lovers*
After three days the blush is gone.

tana *n.f.* den, cave, pit, nest.
Lu pitittu fa nesciri la serpi di la tana.
Eng. *Hunger makes the snake leave its den.*
Lit. *Appetite makes the snake come out of the den.*

113

tannu *adv.* then, at that time.
Tannu si dici bonu lu lavuri, quannu avemu a magasenu lu frumentu.
Source: Pitrè, I, 67
Eng. We'll say it's a good crop once the wheat is in the granary.

tàntu *adj.* many, much, great, much more.
Tanti ervi cc' è, tanti mali avemu. Source: Pitrè, IV, 31.
Eng. Many grasses, many allergies.

tantu quantu *adv.* a little bit.
D'un avaru un tantu quantu;
D'un manciuni 'un cci nn' è nenti. Source: Pitrè, IV, 121.
Eng. A little bit from a miser;
Nothing from a glutton.

taràntula *n.f.* spider.
A 'na manu la taràntula, e a l'àutra la furmicula. Source: Pitrè, III, 192.
Eng. On one hand the spider and on the other the ant.

tardu *adv.* late.
Megghiu tardu ca mai.
Eng. Better late than never.

Quannu lu tardu 'mpara pigghia ed ardilu (**Madonie**). Source: Pitrè, I, 60.
Eng. When the grain grows too slowly pull it out and burn it.

tastari *v.t.* taste, sample, savor.
Tastannu tastannu si rumpi lu dijunu. Source: Pitrè, I, 25.
Eng. Little transgressions lead to the breaking of the law.

tastu *n.m.* mus. key, ivory.
A lu tuccari di li tasti si conusci lu bonu organista. Source: Pitrè, III, 301.
Eng. The touch of the keys reveals the good organist.

taverna *n.f.* tavern, inn, eating house.
Un' ura di taverna leva un annu di malincunia. Source: Pitrè, I, 74.
Eng. One hour at a tavern makes up for a year of melancholy.

tàvula *n.f.* plank, dining table.
A tavula nun s'invecchia.

Eng. One doesn't get old at the table.

A tavulu si scordanu li trìvuli.
Eng. You forget your troubles at the dining table.

Quantu si dici in tavula, divi arristari 'ntra la tuvagghia. Source: Traina, 1018.
Eng. All that's said at the dinner table should not be repeated.
Lit. All that's said at the dinner table should be left on the tablecloth.

tèmpira *n.f.* hardening, temper; autumn rains; temple.
Tuttu va a la tempra. Source: Pitrè, IV, 191.
Eng. It all depends on the temper.
Tr. note: Pitrè's text shows the spelling as **tempra** which happens to be the same spelling as in italian. Traina and Piccitto show the spelling as **tèmpira**.

tempu *n.m.* time.
A tempu chi lu tempu 'un era tempu.
Eng. At the time when time was yet not time.

A tempu di li canonaci di lignu o di lu judici surra.
Eng. When hell freezes over.
Lit. At the time when cannons were made of wood or when the magistrate was speechless.

Bon tempu e malu tempu,
Nun dura tuttu tempu. Source: Pitrè, I, 276.
Eng. Neither good time nor bad time
Lasts for all time.

Dacci tempu a la quagghia.
Eng. Don't fret, give things their time.
Lit. Give it time to curdle.

Lu tempu assicuta lu tempu.
Eng. Time marches on.

Lu tempu è medicu.
Eng. Time heals all things.
Lu tempu vola. Source: Pitrè, III, 380.

Eng. *Time flies.*

tempura *n.f.* Ember Days
A li quattru tèmpura di li vinnigni,
Li suli fimmini digni. Source: Pitrè, III, 10.
Eng. *At the four Ember Days of the grape harvest,*
Only the women observe.
Tr. note: Since the grape harvest is in the fall, this must be the Ember Week that occurs after September 14, The Exaltation of the Cross.

A li quattru tèmpura di Natali,
L'omini l'hannu a fari. Source: Pitrè, III, 10.
Eng. *The Four Ember Days of Christmas*
Must be kept by all.
Tr. note: There are three Ember Days; Wednesday, Friday, and Saturday of four Ember Weeks in the liturgical year; in March, June, September and December. The Ember Weeks begin on the Wednesday after Ash Wednesday, after Whitsunday, after September 14, Exaltation of the Cross, and after December 13, S. Lucia's festival day.

tèniri *v.t.* hold, keep, grasp, detain, possess.
Quannu a lu jocu t' ajuta furtuna,
Nun lu canciari, tenitila bona. Source: Pitrè, III, 386.
Eng. *When luck is helping you at your game,*
Don't change it, keep a good hold.

tènniru *adj.* tender, supple.
A gattu vecchiu, surci tinnireddu. Source: Traina, 430; Pitrè I, 141.
Eng. *The foolish are prey for the clever.*
Pitrè adds: "Those who are well practiced in shrewdness look for the young and inexpert."

tentari *v.t.* try, test, tempt.
Fimmina di trenta, lu dimoniu nun la tenta.
Eng. *A woman of thirty is not tempted by the devil.*

Tentari nun noci.
Eng. *There's no harm in trying.*

terra *n.f.* earth, soil, ground, country, land.
A terra comu vai usa comu trovi.

Eng. When in Rome, do as the Romans.

Cu' simina terri forti, avi certu auguriu e sorti. Source: Pitrè, I, 40.
Eng. Who sows the soil well will reap benefits.

Jetta 'n terra ca Diu cuverna.
Eng. Do the seeding and leave the rest to God.

L'omu è di terra e la terra lu chiama. Source: Pitrè, IV, 379.
Eng. Dust thou art and unto dust shalt thou return.

Terra caura nun fa fretta.
Eng. Good soil, no anxiety.

Tinta dda terra chi lu so patruni nun vidi, e sta 'mputiri di viddani.
Eng. Woe the land that's not overseen by the owner and relies on the peasant.

Tantu vali la terra, quantu l'omu chi la cultiva.
Eng. The worth of the land is determined by the man who cultivates it.

terzu *adj.* third.
A la terza si libbira. Source: Pitrè, I, 309.
Eng. The third time's the charm.
Lit. On the third time it's easy.

testa *n.f.* head, intellect, good sense.
A cu' nun havi testa cci vonnu boni gammi.
Eng. Think ahead or suffer the consequences.
Lit. Those who don't have a head need strong legs.

Di la testa feti lu pisci. Source: Pitrè, II, 337.
Eng. The problem starts at the top.
Lit. The stench of the fish starts at the head.
Tr. note: This proverb is in Pitrè, Volume II, Chapter 46, Government, Laws, National Interest.

Dui cosi nun potti addrizzari lu Signuri, cucuzzi longhi e testa di viddani.
Eng. Two things that the Lord could not straighten, the long squash and the head of the peasant..

Tr. note: Peasants were thought to be obstinate.

La testa di l'omu dottu, morte parra.
Eng. *The works of the scholar continue to speak after his death.*

Testa ch' 'un parra, si chiama cucuzza. Source: Pitrè, III, 233.
Eng. *The head that doesn't speak is called a pumpkin.*

testamentu *n.m.* will, testament.
Grossi spisi e magru testamentu. Source: Traina, 1026.
Eng. *A lot of spending and a meagre estate.*

tila *n.f.* cloth.
A lustru di cannila, nè fimmini nè tila.
Eng. *Don't choose a woman or cloth by candlelight.*

Fimmina e tila 'un si nn'accàttanu di sira.
Eng. *Women and cloth should not be bought in the evening.*

Puddicini e tili, nigozii di fimmini. Source: Pitrè, IV, 245.
Eng. *Tending chicks and making cloth are women's work.*

timogna *n.f.* pile, stack.
Tutti li spichi nun vannu a timogna.
Eng. *Not all the kernels of wheat make it to the wheat pile.*

timpesta *n.f.* storm, tempest.
Acqua, e no timpesta. Source: Pitrè, IV, 113.
Eng. *We want rain, not a storm.*

Bunazza nun c'è mai senza timpesta.
Eng. *There is never a calm sea without a storm.*

Doppu la timpesta veni la calma.
Eng. *The calm after the storm.*

timpirateddu *adj.* watered-down, wishy-washy.
Timpirateddu ti vivi lu vinu,
Ca ti manteni lu stomacu 'n tonu. Source: Pitrè, IV, 142.
Eng. *Drink wine slightly mixed with water*

To promote stomach tone.

timpuni *n.m., pl. timpuna.* sod, clump, farm fields.
Cu' scippa timpuna, mancia cudduruna.Source: Pitrè, 1, 39.
Eng. *Who clears fields eats focaccio.*
Tr. note: Eating focaccia means eating well as a result of earning more by having cleared more land for farming.

timuri *n.m.* fear, dread, awe, apprehension.
Cu' havi timuri di ciàuli 'un simina linu. Source: Pitrè, III, 238.
Eng. *Who worries about magpies won't seed flax.*

Si fussi pri timuri di l'oceddi, nuddu siminiria granu. Source: Pitrè, III, 243.
Eng. *Were it for fear of the birds eating the seeds, nobody would sow grain.*

tinciri *v.t.* color, dye, darken, soil, blemish, defame, defraud, deceive.
Fimmina chi t'abbrazza e strinci,
O t'ha tinciuto o cerca di tinciriti (**Catania**). Source: Pitrè, II, 65.
Eng. *A woman who hugs and squeezes you,*
Has deceived you or is seeking to deceive you.

tintu *adj.* dyed, not good, bad, wicked, naughty, inept, corrupt, putrid.
Frivareddu è curtuliddu, ma nun c'è cchiù tintu d'iddu.
Eng. *February may be short but there's none worse.*

Prestu, tintu. Source: Pitrè, III, 367.
Eng. *Haste makes waste.*

Tantu sta la robba tinta 'n chiazza, sina chi veni lu tintu e si l' accatta.
Eng. *Bad goods will remain in the stall, until a bad shopper buys it all.*
Lit. *Poor goods will stay in the square until an inept shopper comes and buys it.*

tinuta *n.f.* holding, territory, colony.
Cu lu rigàlu d'un bon gaddinazzu,
Di la tinuta patruni ti fazzu. Source: Pitrè, I, 43.
Eng. *With the gift of a good turkey,*
I'll make you the boss of a holding.
Tr. note: When a latifondia, a land management technique introduced by the

Romans, was planted in cereal, it was customary in feudal times, to break the area into manageable territories that would be leased to individual farmers. The farmers would compete to get the best territory, by giving the latifondia steward whatever gifts they could manage.

tirannia *n.f.* tyranny.
'Un amari a cu' t'ama è tirannia.
Eng. *Not loving the one who loves you is tyranny.*

tirari *v.t.* throw, hurl, fling, pull, tug.
La carni tira. Source: Bellantonio, II 149.
Eng. *Blood is thicker than water.*

Megghiu una vota tira tira, ca tanti voti cazza cazza.
Eng. *Better one energetic effort than a hundred half-hearted.*

Non ad ogni cani ch' abbaja s' havi a tirari la petra. Source: Pitrè, II, 405.
Eng. *You don't have to throw a stone at every dog that barks.*

Tirminisi *n.m.* a Tirmini resident.
Tirminisi unu pri paisi;
Quannu nun cci nn' è, megghiu è (**Castelbuono**). Source: Pitrè, IV, 385.
Eng. *One resident of Termini per city;*
When there are none. it's better yet.

tirrenu *n.m.* terrain, land, soil, ground, area.
È sempri cu l'amaru 'mmiscatu l'amuri tirrenu.
Eng. *Love is always bittersweet.*
Lit. *Love's terrain is always mixed with bitterness.*

Nun ti lassari pigghiari un palmu di tirrenu. Source: Pitrè, IV, 171.
Eng. *Don't let anyone take the tiniest bit of your land.*
Tr. note: A **palmu** measured 25.7 centimeters, or about 10 inches.

tirrozzu *n.m.* poor land, unfertilized, uncultivated.
Tirrozzu; fazzu quantu pozzu. Source: Pitrè, I, 69.
Eng. *Poor land; I'll do what I can.*

tirzana *adj.* intermittent, med. paroxysmal .
Frevi tirzana nun sona campana. Source: Pitrè, IV, 13.
Eng. *An intermittent fever is not fatal.*

Lit. An intermittent fever doesn't ring the [church] bell.

tisoru *n.m.* treasure.
L'acqua è oru, la mmerda è tisoru. Source: Pitrè, IV, 260.
Eng. Water is gold, manure is a treasure.
Pitrè explains, for those of us removed from farming, that excrement or manure is a great fertilizer. As you drive through the Central Valley of California you see billboards that simply say, "Water makes things grow." In Bavaria we used to see the farmers fertilize their fields using what we euphemistically called "Honey buckets". They were very large barrel shaped vessels with liquified manure.

tistamentu *n.m.* will, testament.
Fa' tistamentu quannu manci maccarruna a stufatu. Source: Pitrè, III 378.
Eng. Prepare your last will and testament in the fullness of your health.

tistardu *n.m.* obstinate, stubborn.
Cu' è tistardu, va di mali 'n peju. Source: Pitrè, III, 184.
Eng. A stubborn person goes from bad to worse.

tistimonìu *n.m.* testimony, witness.
Vali cchiù un tistimoniu di visu, chi centu d'oricchia. Source: Pitrè, III, 310.
Eng. The testimony of one eyewitness is worth more than a hundred hearsay witnesses.

tistuni *adj., n.m.* stubborn, stubborn person, blockhead, intelligent.
Nna li cosi cci voli testa e tistuni e diavulu chi ti porta. Source: Bellantonio, II 192.
Eng. Day to day you need a good head, stubborness, and good fortune.

tiurìa *n.f.* theory.
La prattica fa cchiù di la tiuria. Source: Bellantonio, II 129.
Eng. You learn more by doing than by listening.
Lit. Practice does more than theory.

tizzuni *n.m.* a charred piece of wood, an ember, an Arab.
Nun cc' è tizzuni senza fumu. Source: Pitrè, III, 93.
Eng. Nobody is perfect.
Lit. There's no ember without smoke.

tocca *v.t.* . draw near, devolve, rightfully have.

Tocca a tìa difinnìrimi.
Eng. *It's up to you to defend me.*

tostu *adj.* cheeky, impudent, unruly, stubborn.
A tavula cci voli facci tosta. Source: Pitrè, IV, 82.
Eng. *At the table you should eat with gusto.*
Lit. *At the table you need to be shameless.*

Facci tosta, e 'un aviri paura. Source: Pitrè, III, 241.
Eng. *Put on a brave front and don't be afraid.*

tozzu *n.m.* morsel, piece; hardened; leftovers, scrap; pebble; smidgen.
A la casa di lu massariotu s' 'un cc' è pani cc' è tozzu. Source: Pitrè, IV, 244.
Eng. *In the farmer's house there's always sustenance.*
Lit. *In the house of the farmer, if there isn't bread, there are leftovers.*

tradimentu *n.m.* treason.
Nun cc' è ventu senza tradimentu. Source: Pitrè, IV, 383.
Eng. *An ill wind blows no good.*

tradituri *n.m.* traitor.
La vucca è traditura di lu cori. Source: Pitrè, III, 223.
Eng. *The mouth betrays the heart.*

tradutturi *n.m.* translator.
Tradutturi, tradituri.
Eng. *Translator, traitor.*

traficari *v.t.* deal, do, act.
Cu' havi dinari, trafica. Source: Pitrè, III, 258.
Eng. *Who has money wheels and deals.*

tramari *v.t* weave, weft, fig. intrigue, plot.
Cui trama 'ngannu,
Cci veni lu dannu. Source: Pitrè, IV, 218.
Eng. *He who plots deceit*
Invites trouble.

tramuntana *n.f.* North Wind.

Sciloccu chiaru e tramuntana scura,
Mèttiti a mari senza paura. Source: Pitrè, III, 66.
Eng. *With a clear Sirocco and a dark North Wind,*
Go to sea without fear.

Tramuntana o tri jorna o 'na simana. Source: Pitrè, III, 70.
Eng. *The North Wind, rain either for three days or for a week.*

tramutari *v.t.* transfer, transport, move; squeeze grapes a second time, make wine turbid from agitation.
Vinu tramutatu
Stà quaranta jorna malatu. Source: Pitrè, IV, 143.
Eng. *Wine that's been moved*
Must rest for forty days.
Tr. note: Nowadays wine makers pass wine through elaborate filters.

trappitu *n.m.* the olive press.
Lupa ppi santu Vitu, puoi chiudiri 'u trappitu.
Eng. *With a dense fog on the feast of St. Vitus (June 15), close the olive press.*

trasiri *v.i.* enter, interfere, penetrate.
Casa unni 'un trasi lu suli, trasi lu medicu. Source: Pitrè, IV, 6.
Eng. *The house not entered by the sun is entered by the doctor.*

Trasi cu Diu e nesci cu lu diavulu. Source: Pitrè, IV, 72.
Eng. *Enter a saint, leave a devil.*
Tr. note: This proverb is in Chapter 79 on Lying and Hypocrisy.

travagghiari *v.t.* work.
Ammatula fai lu mussu a funcia, prima si travagghia e poi si mancia.
Eng. *It's useless to pout; first you work, and then you eat.*

Cui cchiù sapi, cchiù travagghia. Source: Pitrè, IV, 37.
Eng. *He who knows more gets more work.*

L'omu travagghiaturi sempri mancia. Source: Pitrè, III, 197.
Eng. *The man who's a willing worker always eats.*

travagghiu *n.m.* labor, activity, work.

Lu vôi sapiri cosa è lu megghiu?
Circari notti e jornu lu travagghiu. Source: Pitrè, III, 208.
Eng. *Would you like to know what's the best thing?*
To look for work all day and night.
Tr. note: Pitrè says that in October of 1870, he saw this proverb on the house of an iron worker of Acireale, who had become well-off through his work.

trenta *adj.* thirty.
Cui di vinti nun sa, di trenta nun fà, di quaranta nun ha, nè mai sapirà, nè mai farà, nè mai avrà.
Eng. *If you don't know by age twenty, don't do by age thirty, don't have by age forty, you will never know, never do, and never have.*

triaca *n.f.* ancient poison snake bite remedy, dregs, mud, fear.
Acqua senza vinu 'ntra lu corpu è vilenu; vinu senz' acqua 'n corpu è triaca.
Eng. *Water without wine in the body is poison; wine without water in the body is a poison snake bite remedy.*

triacali *adj. inv.* distilled.
L'acqua triacali
Nun fa beni e mancu mali;
Jinchi lu culu a li spiziali. Source: Pitrè, IV, 14.
Eng. *Distilled water*
Does neither harm nor good;
It enriches the pharmacists.
Tr. note: Pitrè adds, Namely, to say it in a clean version, it fills the pockets of the pharmacists.

tribbulazzioni *n.f.* affliction, tribulation, suffering.
La tribbulazzioni è spiruni pri fari beni.
Eng. *An affliction is a spur to do well.*

trincianti *n.m.* carving knife, arch. trenchant.
A la mè robba 'un cci vogghiu trincianti. Source: Bellantonio, II 23.
Eng. *For my things there's no need for a carving knife.*
Tr. note This is an expression of greed.

trintina *n.f.* thirties.
Fimmina trintina,
Jèttala a la marina. Source: Pitrè, II, 79.

Eng. *A woman in her thirties,*
Throw her in the sea.

tristu *adj.* unhappy, sad, aching, evil, wicked, corrupt.
Iri di tristu a pocu bonu.
Eng. *Going from bad to worse.*

trizziatu *v.t. past p.* teased.
Vecchiu 'nnamuratu, di tutti è trizziatu. Source: Pitrè, II, 309.
Eng. *When an old man falls in love he is teased by everyone.*

tronu *n.m.* thunder; throne; toilet.
Lu bonu, un tronu;
Lu santu un lampu. Source: Pitrè, IV, 220.
Eng. *For the good man, a throne;*
For the saint, a votive candle.

trubbula *v.t.* . muddies.
Una stizza di sangu trubbula lu mari.
Eng. *A bit of compassion makes all the difference.*
Lit. *A drop of blood muddies the sea.*

trummetta *n.f.* trumpet, cornet, trumpeter.
La campana è la trummetta di la sepurtura. Source: Pitrè, IV, 181.
Eng. *The church bell is the trumpeter of the grave.*

truniari *v.i.* thunder.
Lu manciari senza viviri
È comu lu truniari senza chiòviri. Source: Pitrè, IV, 97.
Eng. *Eating without drinking*
Is like thunder without rain.

truscia *n.f.* bundle.
Quannu veni di mari,
Pigghia la trùscia e vattinni a lavari. Source: Pitrè, III, 57.
Eng. *When you come from the sea,*
Pick up your bundle and go wash.

truzzari *v.t.* bump, butt, clash, collide with.
Truzza, martinu, ca la Pasqua veni. Source: Pitrè, III, 71.

Eng. *Frolic while you still can, little lamb, for Easter is nigh.*
Pitrè notes that **Martinu** is the name given to the lamb destined for the Easter table.

tuccari *v.t.* touch, handle, feel.
A li parenti, nun fari nenti;
A li vicini, comu li spini;
A li cummari, nun tuccari. Source: Pitrè, III, 314.
Eng. *Leave your relatives alone;*
Treat your neighbors with respect;
Hands off your wife's girlfriends.
Tr. note: This refers to the behavior that a husband may have with other women.

tumazzu *n.m.* cheese.
A tumazzu vecchiu 'un cci pò sali. Source: Bellantonio, II, 208.
Eng. *You can't teach an old dog new tricks.*
Lit. *You can't salt old cheese.*

tuppulìari *v.i.* knock.
Nun tuppuliari a porti firmati (**Marsala**). Source: Pitrè, IV, 173.
Eng. *Don't knock on locked doors.*

turcu *n.m.* unbeliever.
O tutti turchi, o tutti cristiani. Source: Pitrè, III, 386.
Eng. *Either all unbelievers or all Christians.*
Tr. note: This proverb is in Pitrè, Volume III, Chapter 74, Resolve, Solicitude, Seize The Day.

turmentu *n.m.* torment, physical pain, harassment, agony.
Frumenti, turmenti. Source: Pitrè, IV, 226.
Eng. *Farming of grains is at the mercy of nature.*
Lit. *Grains, torments.*

ubbidienza *n.f.* obedience.
La pronta ubbidienza,
È d'ogni virtù la simenza. Source: Pitrè, III, 248.
Eng. *Ready obedience*
Is the kernel of every virtue.

ubbligatu *v.t.* obliged, constrained.
Nuddu è ubbligatu a 'nfamari a sè stissu. Source: Bellantonio, II 233.

Eng. You are not obliged to incriminate yourself.

ugnu *n.m.* nail, claw.
Di l'ugna si canusci lu liuni.
Eng. You recognize a lion by its claws.

umbra *n.f.* shade, shadow, darkness.
Unni nun cc' è luci, nun cc' è umbra. Source: Pitrè, II, 9.
Eng. Where there's no light, there's no shadow.

ùmmira *n.f.* shadow, shade, darkness.
Si scanta ri l'ùmura so'. Source: Annaro, 226.
Eng. He's afraid of his own shadow.

'un *adv.* not.
'Un campa, 'un mori e l' ògghiu s' ardi. Source: Pitrè, IV, 19.
Eng. He's not living; he's not dying and the oil is burning.
Tr. note: Pitrè says, "More than a proverb, in a proverbial mode: in the proverbial form, this is said about one who has been gravely ill and in a state of agony for a long time."

unni *adv.* where.
Unni nun cc' è principiu, nun cc' è fini. Source: Pitrè, IV, 193.
Eng. Where there's no start, there's no finish.

untari *v.t.* oil.
Cui manìa, s'unta. Source: Pitrè, II 279.
Eng. The one who manages helps himself.
Lit. He who manages, oils his own (palm).
Tr. note: This proverb is in Pitrè, Volume II, Chapter 41, Fraud, Robbery. Like Calogero Sedàra in *The Leopard.*

unza *n.f.* ounce.
Lu latru 'un havi a rubbari menu di triccent' unzi: cent'unzi ppi sarvarisilli, cent'unzi ppi cumpòniri lu judici e cent'unzi ppi passarisilla bona 'ntr' 'a càrzara (**Chiaramonte**). Source: Pitrè, IV, 380.
Eng. The thief needs to steal no less than three hundred ounces: one hundred ounces to save, one hundred ounces to pacify the judge and one hundred ounces to be treated well in jail.

Pr' arricchiri un omu cci voli cent'unzi 'nta li manu e du' anni di mala vita.

Source: Pitrè, II, 285.
Eng. *To get rich, a man needs a hundred ounces in his hand and two years of unprincipled living.*

ura *n.f.* hour.
Quannu l'ura 'un è arrivata,
L'ogghiu santu ti servi pri 'nzalata. Source: Pitrè, IV, 384.
Eng. *When your time has not come,*
Use the holy oil for your salad.

Tri uri dorminu li santi, cincu li mircanti, setti li cumuni e novi li putruni.
Source: Pitrè, IV, 75.
Eng. *Saints sleep three hours, merchants sleep five, ordinary people seven and the lazy sleep nine.*

urvicari *v.t.* inter, bury.
Ognunu urvica a so patri comu megghiu pò.
Eng. *Each one does the best he can.*
Lit. *Each one buries his father as best he can.*

usurariu *n.m.* usurer, loan shark.
Guadagnu fattu cu usura pocu dura.
Eng. *Earnings from usury don't last.*

Nun cridiri ad usurariu binignu. Source: Pitrè, IV, 169.
Eng. *Don't believe a compasionate loan shark.*

utri *n.m. inv.* goatskin wine bottle.
Ddoppu vinnigni utri. Source: Pitrè, III, 386.
Eng. *After the grape harvest, wine.*

uziusu *adj.* idle, aching, doleful
L'uziusu di raru è virtuusu. Source: Pitrè, III, 208.
Eng. *The idler is rarely virtuous.*

vacabbunniannu *v.i.* vagabonding, roaming.
Cui va vacabbunniannu,
Un jornu jirrà dumannannu. Source: Pitrè, III, 199.
Eng. *He who goes roaming*
Will one day go begging.

vai *v.i.* of *iri.* go.
Tantu vai, pri quantu hai.
Eng. *Your value is set by your wealth.*
Lit. *You go for as much as you have.*

valanza *n.f.* scales, balance.
La valanza nun canusci diffirenza tra l'oru e lu chiummu. Source: Pitrè,
I, 320.
Eng. *The scale doesn't know the difference between gold and lead.*
Tr. note: This proverb is in Pitrè, Volume I, Chapter 24, Dealing, Commerce.

vali *adj.* worth, value.
Vali cchiù un jornu di l' omu discretu, chi tutta la vita di lu scioccu. Source:
Pitrè, IV, 48.

129

Eng. *One day of a man with discretion is worth more than a lifetime of a fool.*

vanedda *n.f.* street, alley, blind alley.
Ogni vanedda spunta a la Marina (**Catania**). Source: Pitrè, IV, 173.
Eng. *Every street ends up at the Marina.*

vasata *n.f.* kiss.
La prima vasata è la biddizza. Source: Pitrè, IV, 215.
Eng. *The first kiss is the beauty.*

La vasata è lu veru signu di l'amuri. Source: Pitrè, IV, 215.
Eng. *The kiss is the true sign of love.*

vasciu *adj.* low, short.
Li mura vasci sèrvinu a tutti. Source: Pitrè, IV, 222.
Eng. *Fences make good neighbors.*
Lit. *Low walls serve all.*

vasinnò *adv.* otherwise.
Patruna la mogghi e cuntu 'un cci faciti,
Vasinnò sempri in debbitu vi stati. Source: Pitrè, IV, 383.
Eng. *Manage your wife and don't give her account access,*
Otherwise you'll always be in debt.

vassalu *n.m.* vassal, subject.
Un signuri di pagghia si mancia un vassallu d'azzàru. Source: Pitrè, I, 86.
Eng. *A lord made of straw can eat up a vassal made of steel.*
Tr. note: A proverb that aptly expresses the hierarchy of feudal times.

vastuneddu *dim. of vastuni.* stick.
Lu vastuneddu 'nsigna lu garzuneddu. Source: Pitrè, I, 294.
Eng. *The stick teaches the boy.*

vasu *n.m.* vessel, vase, jar; kiss.
Lu bonu vasu fa lu bonu vinu. Source: Pitrè, IV, 137.
Eng. *A good vessel makes good wine.*

Vattiri *v.t.* beat, hit, punch, throb.
Megghiu essiri vattutu di vastuni, chi laciratu di mala lingua. Source:

Pitrè, II, 403.
Eng. *Better to be beaten with a stick than torn apart by gossip.*

vecchia *n.f.* old lady, old woman.
La vecchia 'un voli jocu, voli pani, vinu e focu. Source: Pitrè, II, 301.
Eng. *The old woman doesn't want fun; she wants bread, wine, and warmth.*
Tr. note: This proverb is in Pitrè, Volume II, Chapter 43, Youth, Old Age.

vecchiu *n.m.* old, venerable.
Acqua e ventu, supra la casa di lu vecchiu. Source: Pitrè, III, 4.
Eng. *The trials and tribulations of the old.*
Lit. *Water and wind on the old man's house.*

Vecchiu è cu' mori.
Eng. *The old is the one who dies.*

velenu *n.m.* poison, venom.
Cu' cumponi lu velenu, la prima tazza è la sò.
Eng. *He who compounds a poison, drinks the first cup.*

vència *n.f.* vendetta.
La vència si fa a la sfrattata di li tenni. Source: Pitrè, III, 250.
Eng. *The vendetta is used at the end.*

vèniri *v.i.* come, arrive, reach.
Ben vegna cu' beni porta.
Eng. *The bearer of gifts is welcomed.*

Di lu sapiri si veni a l' aviri. Source: Pitrè, IV, 40.
Eng. *From knowing comes having.*

D'un disordini nni vennu centu. Source: Pitrè, IV, 181.
Eng. *From one mess come a hundred.*
Tr. note: This proverb is in Pitrè, Volume IV, Chapter 89, General sentences.

Li dinari vannu e vennu. Source: Pitrè, I, 157; III, 265.
Eng. *Easy come easy go.*
Lit. *Money comes and goes.*

Vènniri *n.m.* Friday. Also: **vènnari, viènari.**

Cu' arrobba di vènnari 'un è piccatu. Source: Bellantonio, II 198.
Eng. *Who steals on Friday doesn't sin.*
Tr. note: Pitrè doesn't say anything about the variation in spelling.

Lu vènnari è di natura:
Comu agghiorna, accussì scura. Source: Pitrè, III, 38.
Eng. *Friday's weather doesn't change:*
As it dawns, so it sets.
Tr. note: This proverb appears in Pitrè's chapter on Weather. Pitrè says this proverb expresses one of the many prejudices about Friday.

ventri *n.m. n.f.* stomach, belly, womb.
Basta chi lu ventri sia chinu, o di pagghia, o di vinu. Source: Traina, 1080.
Eng. *It's enough when the stomach is full, be it of hay or of wine.*

Birritta di villutu e ventri di liutu. Source: Pitrè, IV, 130.
Eng. *A velvet cap but a stomach that plays the lute.*
Tr. note: The velvet cap is contrasted with the growling stomach. Pitrè explains that the stomach playing the lute means that it's empty. He then quotes another proverb that he says is identical. I've translated it under the keyword **zagareddi**.

ventu *n.m.* wind.
Bisogna jiri cu lu ventu. Source: Pitrè, III, 288.
Eng. *You need to sail with the wind.*

Bisogna navicari cu bonu ventu,
Pri nun jiri a traversu, o ruttu, o avvintu. Source: Pitrè, III, 288.
Eng. *You need to sail with a good wind*
To not lose ground, or be smashed or exhausted.

Cu' chiama ventu lu granu cci spagghia.
Eng. *Called forth, the wind will winnow the grain.*

verità *n.f.* truth.
La verità veni 'n summa comu l'ogghiu.
Eng. *The truth will out.*
Lit. *Truth comes to the surface like oil.*
Tr. note: Also see viritá.

vèrtuli *n.pl.* saddlebags
Cori cuntenti e li vèrtuli 'n coddu. Source: Pitrè, I, 75.

Eng. A happy heart and the saddle bags on his shoulder.

veru *adj.* true.
Lu veru surdu è chiddu chi nun voli sèntiri. Source: Pitrè, I, 296.
Eng. The truly deaf is the one who doesn't want to hear.

vespru *n.m.* vespers, sixth canonical hour.
Lu senti a vespri ca sona?
Eng. Do you understand?
Lit. Do you hear the Vespers sounding?

Ntra vespru e nona nun nesci nudda persuna bona.
Eng. No good person goes out between Vespers and Nones.

Vespru Sicilianu.
Eng. The War of the Sicilian Vespers. The revolution and massacre of 1282 that started during the hour of Vespers to rid Sicily of the reign of Charles of Anjou.

viaggiu *n.m.* voyage, trip, travel, tour.
Amari la sò vicina è gran vantaggiu,
Spissu si vidi, e nun si fa viaggiu. Source: Pitrè, I, 101.
Eng. It's a great advantage to love someone in your neighborhood; You see each other often, and you don't have to travel.

Fari un viaggiu è du' sirvizza.
Eng. Kill two birds with one stone.
Lit. Making a voyage that serves two purposes.

viaticu *n.m.* viaticum.
Nun nesci viaticu senza tammurinu (**Castelvetrano**). Source: Pitrè, IV, 247.
Eng. The viaticum won't be administered without an offering.

Vicarìa *n.f.* Vicaria, jail, main prison of the Viceroys.
Avissi ed **avirria**, unu morsi 'mpisu e l' àutru 'ntra la vicarìa. Source: Pitrè, I. 12.
Eng. If I had and I should have, one died by hanging and the other in jail.

vicchiaja *n.f.* old age. Also: **vicchiaia**.

A la vicchiaja ogni fatiga è pisu. Source: Bellantonio, II, 207.
Eng. In old age every task is onerous.

vicchizza *n.f.* old age.
A li vicchizzi cutiddati. Source: Bellantonio, II, 208.
Eng. With old age comes pain.

vicini *n.pl.* neighbors.
Cu vicini e cu parenti nun cci accattari e vinniri nenti.
Eng. With neighbors or relatives. buy or sell nothing.

vicinu *n.m.* neighbor.
Lu malu vicinu è amicu fintu. Source: Pitrè, I, 221.
Eng. A bad neighbor is a false friend.

Quannu si' pri caminu, nun diri mali di lu tò vicinu.
Eng. When you're around about. don't speak poorly of your neighbor.

viddanu *n.m.* peasant, hired hand, rude, ill mannered.
A lu viddanu la zappa 'm manu.
Eng. Each to his own work.

A lu viddanu nun ci dari bacchetta 'm manu.
Eng. Never give authority to a churlish or unqualified person.

E unni mai si 'ntisi viddanu gentili e marinaru curtisi?
Eng. Where did anyone ever hear of a polite peasant and a courteous sailor?

La terra si fa pi lu viddanu. Source: Bonner, 86.
Eng. The earth is made for the peasant.
Meaning: Refers to the old social order in Sicily where people who were born into a particular station generally could never get out of it. English translation by Bonner.

Lu viddanu è comu lu pannu, chi mai lassa la sò piega.
Eng. The peasant will always be a country bumpkin.
Lit. The peasant is like a wrinkle that won't come out of clothing.

viddicu *n.m.* umbilical cord, navel.
Nasciri cu lu viddicu d'oru.

Eng. Born with a silver spoon in his mouth.
Lit. To be born with an umbilical cord of gold.

vìdiri *v.t.* see. Also: **vidiri.**
Viristi u' suri a quatrètti? Source: Annaro, 233.
Eng. Were you in jail?
Lit. Did you see the sun through the squares (of the fence)?

Zoccu nun si vidi, nun è di fidi. Source: Bellantonio, II 189.
Eng. That which is not seen is not believed.

vigghia *v.i.* awake.
Cu' vigghia, la pigghia. Source: Traina, 1087.
Eng. The early bird catches the worm.
Lit. He who wakes, takes.

Quannu lu jornu 'n peni si travagghia, pri li pinseri la notti si vigghia.
Eng. When you work with anxiety during the day, you'll awaken at night with your thoughts.

viggilia *n.f.* vigil, eve.
Prumettiri e nun dari, nun si pò fari. Source: Pitrè, III, 285.
Eng. Promising and not giving, can't be done.
Pitrè notes, "Because:" (see the next proverb.)

Prumettiri è vigilia di lu dari. Source: Pitrè, III, 285.
Eng. Promising is the vigil of giving.
Tr. note: It precedes and is followed by giving.

viggilia ammucciàta *n.f.* hypocrite, liar.
Diu ti scanzi di focu sutta cinniri e di vi gilia ammucciata. Source: Pitrè, IV, 67.
Eng. God preserve you from embers under ashes and a hypocrite.
Pitrè notes: "*Vigilia ammucciata,* fig. said of a person who is a liar and hypocrite, who is not a model gentleman." Piccitto now defines it as a feminine noun, a single word spelled with a double g, and having the meaning of liar or hypocrite.

vigna *n.f.* vineyard.
Accatta vigna di cu' nu' 'nn'havi chiantata, accatta casa di cu' nu' nn'ha fabbricatu.
Eng. Buy a vineyard from one who didn't plant it and a house from one

135

who didn't build it.

Amara dda vigna chi di pruppaina nun digna.
Eng. *Sorry the vineyard that fails to have sprouts.*

È megghiu stari sulu a la sò vigna, ca la vigna d'autru cunzari.
Eng. *It's better to have your own vineyard than to work on someone else's.*

Olivari di tò nannu, cèusi di tò patri, vigna tò.
Eng. *The olive grove of your grandfather, the cherry trees of your father, and your grape vines.*

Vigna purpaniata, vigna eterna. Source: Pitrè, IV, 385.
Eng. *A propagating vineyard is an eternal vineyard.*

vilenu *n.m.* poison.
Latti e vinu, vilenu finu. Source: Pitrè, IV, 94.
Eng. *Milk and wine together make an excellent poison.*

Lu peju vilenu è chiddu di la lingua. Source: Pitrè, II, 402.
Eng. *The tongue is the worst poison.*

vili *adj.* vile, low, abject, despicable, cowardly.
A cori vili nun giuva la forza. Source: Pitrè, III, 235.
Eng. *Strength doesn't help the faint hearted.*

vinciri *v.t.* win.
L'arti si parti e la natura vinci. Source: Pitrè, III, 123.
Eng. *Talent enters where skill leaves off.*

Lu tempu vinci ogni cosa. Source: Pitrè, IV, 185.
Eng. *Time conquers all.*

vinnigna *n.f.* grape harvest.
Cu' travagghia pri la vinnigna s'arriposa tuttu l'annu. Source: Traina, 1089.
Eng. *The grape harvest enriches.*
Lit. *Who works the grape harvest rests the entire year.*

Prima di la vinnigna, cunzati la vutti! Source: Pitrè, III, 368.

Eng. *Prepare the barrels before the grape harvest.*

vinnitta *n.f.* revenge, vendetta, massacre, carnage.
Ogni pena 'n pani torna,
Cui cu la panza 'un si pigghia vinnitta. Source: Pitrè, I, 77.
Eng. *He who avoids revenge to fill his stomach*
turns every hurt into bread.

vintottu *adj.* twenty-eight.
Chiantarisi cu vintottu. Source: Traina, 1091.
Eng. *To pretend not to know, understand, or be aware of something and*
thereby forego commenting.
Lit. *Stand on twenty-eight.*

vintura *n.f.* luck, chance, risk, destiny.
Cci voli la vintura di Giufà.
Eng. *The luck of Giufà is needed.*
Tr. note: Giufà is a celebrated idiot savant kind of character in Sicilian literature
and folklore who, despite apparent bungling, always came out on top.

Mentri dura, è vintura. Source: Pitrè, III,382.
Eng. *It's good fortune while it lasts.*

Mentri dura, nun è vintura. Source: Pitrè, III, 382.
Eng. *As long as it lasts, it's bad luck.*

vinu *n.m.* wine.
A pocu vinu, vivi primu. Source: Pitrè, III, 371.
Eng. *When there's little wine, be among the first to drink.*

Carni fa carni, pani fa panza, vinu fa danza. Source: Pitrè, IV, 84.
Eng. *Meat makes meat, bread makes a paunch, and wine makes you dance.*

Lu bonu vinu dura sinu a la fezza.
Eng. *Good wine lasts down to the dregs.*

Lu vinu è lu latti di li vecchi. Source: Pitrè, IV, 140.
Eng. *Wine is the milk of the old.*

Lu vinu nun appi mai frenu.

Eng. *The drunkard loses all inhibitions.*

Nun ti mettiri in camminu, si la tua vucca nun sapi lu vinu.
Eng. *Don't go on your way if the wine you didn't assay.*

Vinu amaru tenilu caru. Source: Pitrè, IV, 143.
Eng. *Integrity is priceless.*
Lit. *Bitter wine, value it dearly.*

vipara *n.f.* viper, adder, snake
La vìpara dici: 'un mi tuccari, ca 'un ti toccu;
Ma si mi tocchi, iu ti stoccu. Source: Pitrè, IV, 242.
Eng. *The viper says: don't touch me, and I won't touch you;*
But if you touch me, I'll strike you.

virdi *adj.* green, grass, greenery.
Nun sempri virdi si manteni un citru.
Eng. *This too shall pass.*
Lit. *A citron doesn't stay green forever.*

Pani càudu, ligna virdi e mugghieri picciotta. Source: Pitrè, IV, 103.
Eng. *Warm bread, green wood, and a young wife.*

virga *n.f.* stick, crop, shepherd's crook, baton.
Li virghi nun si rumpinu tutti nzemmula.
Eng. *In union there is strength.*
Lit. *Sticks can't be broken when they're together.*

virrutu *adj.* angry, furious, aggressive.
Fatti virrutu, ca sarai timutu. Source: Pitrè, III, 241.
Eng. *Act aggressive so that you will be feared.*

virtù *n.f.* virtue. *Also: virtuti.*
La virtù è 'na bedda picciotta e tutti l'amanu, ma pochi 'n casa cci acchia-nanu. Source: Pitrè, IV, 146.
Eng. *Virtue is a beautiful young woman that everyone loves, but few can climb to her house.*

A bonu locu stannu li virtù. Source: Pitrè, IV, 145.

Eng. *The virtues are well situated.*
La furtuna leva e duna,
Ma cu la virtù nun havi forza alcuna. Source: Bellantonio, II 193.
Eng. *Good fortune comes and goes,*
But it has nothing to do with virtue.

La virtù e la virità vennu sempri 'nsumma comu l'ògghiu. Source: Pitrè,
IV, 58.
Eng. *Virtue and truth always come to the top like oil.*

Mentri si' 'n giuventù acquìstati virtù. Source: Pitrè, II, 306.
Eng. *Acquire virtue while you're young.*
Tr. note: This proverb is in Pitrè, Volume II, Chapter 43, Youth, Old Age.

Nun cc'è virtù chi puvirtà nun guasta. Source: Pitrè, III, 263.

Eng. *There is no virtue that is not laid waste by poverty.*

virtuusamenti *adv.* virtuously.
Megghiu viviri virtuusamenti, chi nasciri nobilmenti Source: Pitrè, I, 84.
Eng. *It's better to live virtuously than to be nobly born.*

viscottu *n.m.* biscuit, necessity, preparation.
Nun t'immarcari senza viscottu. Source: Traina, 1095.
Eng. *Don't embark without preparation.*

vista *n.f.* sight, view.
La vista soli 'ngannari.
Eng. *You can't judge a book by its cover.*
Tr. note: Appearance can fool you.

vistutu *adj.* dressed, clothed, endowed.
Centu vistuti nun ponnu spugghiari a unu nuru.
Eng. *One hundred who are clothed can't undress one who is naked.*

Cui nasci vistutu è furtunatu. Source: Pitrè, III, 259.
Eng. *He is fortunate who is born affluent.*

vita *n.f.* life.
La robba e la vita sta 'n putiri di Diu.
Eng. *God has dominion over your possessions and your life.*

La vita di l'omu è curta e travagghiata.
Eng. *Life is short and troubled.*

La vita umana è simili a la rosa.
Eng. *Our life is similar to that of the rose.*

viteddu *m.* calf, veal, calfskin, seal.
Corda fa viteddu, zimma fa purceddu, costa fa agneddu, para fa ciavareddu. Source: Piccitto, V, 1159; Pitrè, I, 125.
Eng. *Keep the calf tied, the piglet in the sty, the lamb in the pasture and the goat in a pen.*
Tr. note: Advice on the best way to raise newborn animals. According to a note referencing Mina-Palumbo.
viti *n.f.* grapevine.

Dici la viti fammi poviru ca ti fazzu riccu.
Eng. *The vine says, make me poor and I'll make you rich.*
Tr. note: Make the vine poor by pruning it vigorously.

viulentu *adj.* violent.
Cosa viulenti pocu dura. Source: Pitrè, IV, 115.
Eng. *A violent thing has a short duration.*

viviri *v.t.* drink.
Lu sceccu porta vinu e vivi acqua. Source: Pitrè, I, 267.
Eng. *The jackass carries wine and drinks water.*
Tr. note: But the cart drivers drink wine. See the proverb under **Chiuppu.**

Nun si pò fari viviri lu sceccu pri forza. Source: Pitrè, I, 21.
Eng. *You can take a horse to water, but you can't make it drink.*
Lit. *You can't force a donkey to drink.*

viviri *v.i.* live.
Cu' pensa viviri longu tempu, vivi mali. Source: Pitrè, III, 102.
Eng. *He who thinks he'll have a long life lives recklessly.*

vizziusu *adj.* depraved, iniquitous, gluttonous, fussy, picky at eating.
Lu viziusu 'un havi vrigogna. Source: Pitrè, IV, 154.
Eng. *The decadent has no shame.*

voi *n.m.* ox.
Lu voi non parra ch'ha la lingua grossa, ma si parrassi gran cosi dirrìa.
Source: Pitrè, III, 227.
Eng. *The ox doesn't speak because it can't, but if it could, it would have a lot to say.*

Nun mèttiri lu carru avanti li voi. Source: Pitrè, III, 307.
Eng. *Don't put the cart before the horse.*

volontà *n.f.* will, intent.
A cu' ha mala volontà nun mancanu occasioni. Source: Traina, 1101.
Eng. *The evil minded lack not the occasion.*

vonnu *v.t.* want.
Li ricchi comu vonnu e li poviri comu ponnu. Source: Pitrè, III, 266.

Eng. *The rich do as they want and the poor do as they can.*

voscu *n.m.* forest, woods.
Nè voscu senza ligna, nè aria senza sulami, nè jinia senza corna. Source: Traina, 1102.
Eng. *Neither a forest without trees, nor air without chaff, nor a generation without shame.*

Unni cc'è vòscura cci su' lupi. Source: Pitrè, III, 100.
Eng. *Where there's a forest, there are wolves.*

vozza *n.f.* crop.
Gaddinedda chi cammina, s'arricogghi ccu la vozza china. Source: Zinna, 124.
Eng. *The chicken that ventures forth returns with a full crop.*

vriogna *n.f.* shame, disgrace, insult, honor, good name. ·
Cui perdi la vrigogna nun la trova cchiù. Source: Pitrè, III, 281.
Eng. *Who loses his sense of shame will never regain it.*

Scappari non è virgogna, quacchi vota è sarvamentu di vita. Source: Cipolla, 23.
Eng. *Fleeing is not shameful: sometimes it's life saving.* Trans by Cipolla.

vrodu *n.m.* broth, stock.
Cui mancia carni e cui vivi vrodu,
Tutti cci agghiurnamu la matina di Pasqua. Source: Pitrè, I, 277.
Eng. *In spite of our differences.*
We share a common heritage.
Lit. *Some of us eat meat and some drink broth;*
We all greet Easter morning.

vucca *n.f.* mouth.
A colpu di vucca, scutu d' oricchia.
Eng. *When the mouth speaks, the ear pays heed.*

A vucca chiusa nun ci trasinu muschi.
Eng. *A closed mouth won't catch flies.*

vulinteri *adv.* willingly.

Cui paga vulinteri è riccu. Source: Pitrè, IV, 259.
Eng. *Whoever pays willingly, is rich.*

vuliri *v.t.* want, will, wish, desire.
Li ricchi cchiù chi nn'hannu, cchiù nni vurrianu. Source: Pitrè, III, 266.
Eng. *The more the rich have the more they want.*

Vuliri è putiri. Source: Pitrè, II.
Eng. *Where there's a will, there's a way.*

zagaredda *n.f.* ribbon, binding.
La vesta tutta china di zagareddi
E poi cantanu e sònanu li vudeddi. Source: Pitrè, IV, 130.
Eng. *All decked out in buttons and bows*
And then the stomach is growling.
Lit. *Dress filled with ribbons*
And then the gut is singing and playing.
Tr. note: Pitrè notes that this proverb is the same as the proverb, Birritta di villutu e ventri di liutu, which is translated under the keyword **ventri**. Both proverbs contrast outward appearance with the reality of hunger. An example of Bedda Fiura taken to the extreme because as you will also read under the keyword **ventri**, Ventri affamatu non senti raggiuni.

zanni *n.m.* charlatan, fraud, zany.
Fari lu matrimoniu di lu zanni. Source: Traina, 1113.
Eng. *Pull a fast one.*

zappari *v.t.* hoe.
Cui zappa, zappa la sò vigna,
Cu' bona la zappa, bona la vinnigna (*Alimena*). Source: Pitrè, I, 42.
Eng. *Who hoes, hoes his own vineyard;*
Who hoes well has a good harvest.
Pitrè adds: "Metaphorically it means that those who work for themselves strive to do well."

Unni va Martinu? a zappari lu piru. Source: Pitrè, I, 25.
Lit. *Where is Martin going? He's going to hoe the pear tree.*
Tr. note: Said of a person who always talks about the same happening or often talks about somthing that is dear to him.

zappudda *n.f.* hoe.

La zappudda di jinnaru jinchi lu panaru. Source: Pitrè, I, 50.
Eng. *Hoeing in January will fill the basket.*

zappuna *n.f.* countrywomen, farm women, rural women.
Macàri li zappuna portanu lu circu e lu cantùsciu. Source: Pitrè, IV, 132.
Eng. *Even farm women don crinoline petticoats and long dresses.*
Tr. note: Pitrè supplied the meaning of the antiquated words *zappuna*, *circu*, and *cantùsciu.*
"Zappuna qui detto delle donne de' villici."

zeru *n.m.* zero
Zeru porta zeru:
Tutti cosi a magasenu (**Borgetto**). Source: Pitrè, I, 73.
Eng. *Zero carries zero:*
Everything goes to pay off the debt.
Pitrè adds the following note: Salamone-Marino, to whom this collection owes so much, explains: "This proverb refers mostly to the farmer who brings his produce such as wheat, fava, etc. to the owner, his creditor, and leaves empty handed, with his arms dangling, seeing that his sacks ended up empty."

zimmaru *n.m.* ram, ignoramus.
L'omini su' comu li zimmari: chiddu chi fa unu fannu tutti. Source: Pitrè, IV, 182.
Eng. *Men are like rams: what one does, they all do.*

zita *n.f.* fiancée, sweetheart, bride.
Chista è la zita.
Eng. *What you see is what you get.*
Quannu lu zitu e la zita si vonnu, li parenti accurdari a forza si hannu.
Eng. *When sweethearts want each other the relatives must inevitably accede.*

zitaggiu *n.m.* engagement, marriage, wedding favors, wedding clothing and jewelry.
Ziti vonnu o zitaggi o morti
E festi fora li porti (**Castelvetrano**). Source: Pitrè, IV, 233.
Eng. *Lovers want marriage or death*
And celebrations out of doors.
Tr. note: Also spelled *zittaghju.*

zitu *n.m.* fiance.

Pri sta sira patu patu.
Dumani a sira lu zitu a lu latu. Source: Pitrè, IV, 223.
Eng. For this evening make do.
Tomorrow evening my fiance at my side.

zoccu *pron.* that which, what.
Pani e taci; Zoccu si mancia a tàula 'un si dici. Source: Pitrè, III, 229.
Eng. Bread and silence; What's said at table should not be told.
Lit. What's eaten at the table should not be told.

Zoccu si cumincia, si finisci. Source: Bellantonio, II 20.
Eng. Finish what you start.

Zoccu voli 'na donna fa. Source: Pitrè, II, 123.
Eng. A woman does as she pleases.

zoppu *n.m.* lame.
A zoppu nun ci servi di diri curri.
Eng. It serves no purpose to tell the lame to run.

La vera nova la porta lu zoppu. Source: Pitrè, IV, 57.
Eng. Good news eventually arrives.

Quannu ti vôi fari gabbu di lu zoppu, bisogna chi tu fussi drittu. Source:
Alaimo, 30.
Eng. Men in glass houses should not throw stones.
Lit. Before you make fun of the lame, you yourself need to be upright.

zorba *n.f.* sorb apple.
La primavera fa ciuriri l'erbi,
L'autunnu duci fa cutugna e zorbi. Source: Pitrè, III, 33.
Eng. Springtime brings flowering,
In autumn the quince and sorb apples are sweetening.

zòriu *n.m.* boor, oaf, peasant, lout.
Di tri v'aviti a scantari: di lu diavulu ppi malizia, di li picciriddi ppi 'nnuc-
cenzia, di li zòrii ppi 'gnuranza (***Modica***). Source: Pitrè, IV, 378.
Eng. There are three things to fear: the devil for his malice, tots for their
innocence, boors for their ignorance.

zuccaru *n.m.* sugar, sweets, sweetness.

Cu' ha guastu lu balataru,
Lu zuccaru cci sapi amaru. Source: Pitrè, I, 11.
Eng. *To one with a spoiled palate,*
Sugar seems bitter.
Tr. note: Also **balatu** and **palataru**.

Lu zuccaru fa càdiri li denti. Source: Pitrè, IV, 17.
Eng. *Sugar makes teeth fall out.*

zuccu *n.m..* trunk.
Si dugnu a lu zuccu soffri la rama. Source: Piccitto, IV, 64.
Eng. *If you hurt the father. the children suffer.*
Lit. *If you beat on the trunk, the branch suffers.*

zuccuni *n.m.* trunk, stem, stalk, log, corncob, core, lout, blockhead, igno-
ramus.
Campa zuccuni, chi mori baruni. Source: Pitrè, IV, 35.
Eng. *Live a blockhead. die a baron.*
Tr. note: Pitrè says the proverb is meant as, "A discouragement for anyone who
doesn't want to be an ignoramus."

Zuppiddu *n.m.* Wednesday, Friday, or more often, Thursday before Car-
neval.
Lu Vènnari Zuppiddu
Cui nun ha dinari, mali è pr'iddu. Source: Pitrè, III, 37.
Eng. *Pity the man who has no money*
on the Friday before Mardi Gras.

Bibliography

Alaimo, Emma, *Proverbi Siciliani*, 188 pp, Giunti Gruppo Editoriale, Firenze, 1974, 1991.

Ancona, Vincenzo, *Malidittu La Lingua: Damned Language*, edited by Anna L. Chairetakis & Joseph Sciorra, translated by Gaetano Cipolla, Legas, 1990.

Annaro, Sac. Nunzio, *il "Siciliano" a Caltagirone*, published by sac. Nunzio Annaro, 351pp., Caltagirone, 1993.

Attanasio, Sandro, *Parole Di Sicilia: Frasi, espressioni, detti, paragoni, proverbi e "vastasate"*, 424 pp., Mursia, Milano, 1989.

Arba Sicula, Journal of Sicilian Folklore and Literature, Modern Foreign Languages and Classical Studies, St. John.s University, Jamaica, New York 11439. ed. Gaetano Cipolla.

Bellantonio, Loredana, ed, Pitrè, Giuseppe, *Proverbi Siciliani raccolti e confrontati con quelli degli altri dialetti d'Italia*,Vol. II, a cura di Loredana Bellantonio, Documenta Edizioni S.D.C., Comiso, 2002. (This edition of Volume II of Pitrè's work is listed under the editor's name because the pagination is different than the orignal. The reference in the proverb translations appear as, "Bellantonio, II, nn". The nn is replaced by the page number in this edition.)

Bonner, J.K."Kirk", *Introduction to Sicilian Grammar*, LEGAS, P.O.Box 040328, Brooklyn, NY 11204, 225 pp, 2001.

Camilleri, Andrea, *Il gioco della mosca*, 91 pp., Sellerio editore, Palermo 3rd. ed. 1998.

Cipolla, Gaetano, *What Makes a Sicilian?*, 32 pp., LEGAS, Mineola, 3rd. reprint. 2001.

Copani, Isidoro, *Ammatula si pisca si a l'amu non c'è l'isca: Locuzioni e proverbi di Sicilia (Nuova raccolta)*, 277 pp., c.u.e.c.m. Cooperativa Universitaria Editrice Catanese di Magistro, Catania, 1996.

Fulci, Innocenzio, *Lezioni filologiche sulla lingua siciliana*, 223 pp., Catania, 1855. A grammar in eight lessons, or chapters: History, Pronunciation and orthography, Noun, Pronoun, Verb, Preposition, Adverb and conjunction, Postscript. Followed by notes for each chapter.

Moceo, Pietro, *Semu ricchi e nuddu u sapi*, 173 pp.,Catania, 1855. A grammar in eight lessons, or chapters: History, Pronunciation and orthography, Noun, Pronoun, Verb, Preposition, Adverb and conjunction, Postscript. Followed by notes for each chapter.

Piccitto, Giorgio, ed., *Vocabolario Siciliano*, Vol. I, 973 pp., Catania -- Palermo, 1977. Vol. II, Giovanni Tropea, ed., 938 pp., Catania -- Palermo, 1985. Vol. III, Giovanni Tropea, dir., 1,063 pp., Catania -- Palermo, 1990. Vol. IV, Giovanni Tropea, dir., 886 pp., 1997. Vol. V, Giovanni Tropea, dir., Salvatore C. Trovato, ed., 1,323 pp., Catania -- Palermo, 2002.

Pitrè, Giuseppe, *Proverbi Siciliani raccolti e confrontati con quelli degli altri dialetti d'Italia*,Vol. I, II, III, & IV, Ristampa dell'edizione di Palermo, 1875,

Arnaldo Forni Editore, Sala Bolognese, 1982.

Sutera, Danny, *Some proverbs that his mother taught him*, provided to me via email, 2004.

Traina, Antonino, *Vocabolario Siciliano-Italiano*, 1159 pp., Palermo, 1868, Reprint, s. a. s., undated.

Zinna, Lucio, *Proverbi Siciliani*, 128 pp., Reprint, s. a. s., Palermo, 1995. Sicilian proverbs translated into Italian. A collection of 546 proverbs organized by subject.